The Secret Language of Synchronicity

Deciphering the Words & Wisdom of Meaningful Coincidence

Jenna Moore Fuller

THE SECRET LANGUAGE OF SYNCHRONICITY:
DECIPHERING THE WORDS & WISDOM OF MEANINGFUL
COINCIDENCE

ISBN 978-0-692-56069-3

Manufactured in the United States of America
First printing November 2015

Dedication

For all my wise Watsons, who helped me follow the clues once the game was afoot. And, of course, the big U for providing them.

Table of Contents

Introduction 1

1 - The What, Why, How, Who & When
of Synchronicity 5

2 - Why Synchronicity? Why Words? Why Now? 21

3 - The Beauty & Benefits of Meaningful
Coincidence 33

4 - Types of Synchronicity 47

5 - Thinking, Speaking & the Magic of Words 65

6 - Different Perceptions, Different Preferences
of Words 71

7 - Sight Perceptors & the Written Word 81

8 - Sound Perceptors & the Spoken Word 95

9 - Touch Perceptors & Both Types of Words 101

10 - Lifepath, Passions, & the Joy of Flow 105

11 - Written Word Synchronicities 115

12 - Spoken Word Synchronicities 133

13 - Combination Word Synchronicities 141

14 - Asking & Attracting Meaningful Coincidence 147

15 - Recognizing Synchronicity 151

16 - Understanding Coincidence 173

17 - Extra Helps for Understanding Coincidence 189

18 - Responding to Synchronicity 195

19 - Transformation Through Coincidence 203

20 – Synchronicity – The Final Word 209

References 217

About the Author 220

Introduction

February 2007, Salem OR: The morning is clear and unseasonably warm, and a bit of a breeze from slightly open backseat windows gently cools my face. I am driving through downtown traffic, enjoying the pleasant weather, and also thinking about something else. The subject of synchronicity, to be exact, or "meaningful coincidence," as it is sometimes called. That fascinating phenomena of outward signs or circumstances that seem to somehow answer inner needs and wants.

I've long been intrigued by the occurrences, particularly the WORDS synchronicity uses to convey highly personal messages. And I want to know more. More important, to me anyway, is synchronicity real? Does some Universal force pay attention to our everyday concerns and desires, standing by to help us out? And does it answer us through meaningful coincidence via symbolic or literal words of insight?

So I decide to try a little test. Right then and there while coasting along, I put my questions out to the ethers – "Is synchronicity real?" and "Are signs available to guide us whenever we ask?" Then I try to open my mind to receive, well, whatever.

Approaching an intersection of streets, I pull up to a red light. Simultaneously in the adjoining lane, a van stops alongside. Its side panel advertising, flashy and bold, grabs my attention. "Signs of all types made to order," it boasts, sounding much like cosmic reassurance that this message-making business is no big deal. Jiminy! What just happened here? Is this thing valid? Talk about instant messaging. Just a second between my questions and their answers!

The whole thing seems a bit much – maybe only a fanciful fluke or product of my imagination. Still I wonder, what would happen if I asked again? So I do, and as if on cue another van speeds across the intersection in the opposite direction. "Signs! Signs! Signs!" its advertising shouts out, and my heart skips a beat or two at that. I don't have time to read the small print, but it doesn't really matter. I get the message. Right there, right then, synchronicity rings true for me. It feels powerful, yet it is puzzling, and I want to learn all I can about it.

Fast forward to 2012. During the previous five years, I've often been amazed and impressed by the eclectic variety of meaningful coincidences I've experienced. I've pondered them, deciphered them, and kept careful records of them in my journal. I've acted on them and benefited from studying their symbolism. But important questions still remain. Namely:

1. Do different types of personalities experience

different types of coincidence?

2. Does one personality type experience mostly synchronicities involving written words; another type, spoken words? If so,

3. Will recognizing and understanding our special personal type of coincidental messages lead us to a happier and more meaningful life?

A concurrent dream seems to address my questioning. It features a common symbol, an unexplored house, an image I am familiar with and recognize from previous dreams. In this adventure, I am excited to remember that my house has an enormous upstairs level that I have never completely explored. There is a good feeling of anticipation, as I know it may hold a trove of beautiful and valuable things. I plan a dream-time party to share the treasure hunt with others, and to celebrate our discoveries.

I am happy to recognize this encouraging message which seems to refer to the treasure hunt I am anxious to begin into synchronistic words and their wisdoms, as well as human "upstairs" treasures of mind. The dream leaves me with a happy sense of expectation. It feels like a nocturnal nod and a wink – a kind of confirmation of this beckoning project.

My goals for this book are simple: to record and share my exploration of the phenomena and to serve as a possible catalyst in your own journey of self-discovery. I hope you will join me on this quest to decipher the secret language of synchronicity – the mysterious, the wise, ever personal words of meaningful coincidence.

1

The What, Why, How, Who & When of Synchronicity

The What

Back in the 1950s, when Swiss psychologist Carl Jung originated the term "synchronicity," many people had never heard of him or his research. Most folks, however, were probably aware of unusual instances of his subject of study happening in their own lives. For Jung, synchronicity was a principle in which events happened simultaneously but not causally. The experience often consisted of an inner and outer event, somehow linked, but not as cause and effect. And to the recipient, if felt meaningful. With that sense of significance the episode revealed itself to be far more than happenstance – a true synchronicity.

It seems the events of meaningful coincidence often happen at the same time or close to it. Though there usually isn't much of a gap between them, the understanding of their significance is sometimes delayed. Whether this understanding is intuited instantly or later, however, the perceiver's feeling that these inner and outer events are somehow intertwined and meaningful, is always there.

What are these inner events that can trigger synchronicity? Pretty much any mental state that we as humans experience: thoughts, feelings, visions and dreams. By some means these states spontaneously match up with outward events in the forms of information and circumstances that respond, it appears, in answer.

Typical examples that most of us have experienced include times when we have focused on something physical, maybe a desired object or activity, only to have it quickly and literally show up in our lives. Or a person we think or talk about, who suddenly shows up or communicates with us in some way.

Many of the most fascinating instances of common synchronistic experiences involve the receipt of messages – the exact information we need to answer a question or solve a problem. We might discover a new book, receive a letter, talk to a friend, or overhear the conversation of strangers. In each case the physical things or information we receive will be a perfect fit for our personal requirements. My husband Eric reminds me of this example:

Spring 2012, Salem OR: "This happened during the time I was an active backpacker. I loved everything about it back then – the scenery, the peacefulness, the exercise, the necessary supplies. In fact, keeping up with quality stuff was such an important part of my enjoyment that I was pretty much always on the lookout for some improved piece of equipment or tool to handle a backpacking task a little better. Which brings us to the coincidence."

He continues, "It was spring, and I had been going through my supplies, reviewing needs for upcoming hikes. I wanted to buy and compare an internal frame backpack to the external frame ones I already had. IF I could find one at a bargain. Like for $50, I remember saying, maybe at a yard sale.

"This discussion was going on as we rode with my sister, who was taking us to some event or other in town. The words were barely out of my mouth when we rolled by an enormous outdoor sale. 'Stop the car!' I exclaimed. She did and we all piled out to investigate the wares. Turned out there was a fantastic find for me, an internal frame backpack for sale, coincidentally priced at $50!"

Or another occasion, a simple coincidence of precisely relevant information received through the spoken word.

March 2010, Salem: I am having lunch with my sister-in-law Naomi at a buffet. The restaurant's selection includes a good assortment of salad ingredients as well as several pre-made dishes. One labeled "wasabi salad," looks interesting. "What's wasabi?" Naomi asks. I have a vague concept of it being an ingredient of Japanese cuisine, but though I love international menus I have seldom eaten that type of food.

"Some kind of seaweed?" I venture. "We'll have to look it up later." We try some of the salad with our meals and it is delicious. I promptly forget about our question though. Until the next day when my son Jason calls to chat. I ask what fun he's been up to lately and he mentions going out for sushi – and wasabi.

I feel a quick little tickle of amusement at that, and of course ask him about the word. He explains his understanding, that dishes named for the ingredient are flavored with some kind of pungent root used as a condiment. Clarification information that turns out to be more accurate by far than my seaweed conjecture.

And then an example of one more, an uncomplicated yet relevant coincidence involving desired information delivered via the written word. Eric relates this incident to me:

"My friend Duane had once received an extremely funny cartoon over the Internet. He described it to his wife and explained how he didn't save it then but would like to see it again now." On the other end of the synchronistic teeter-totter, things were apparently shifting. "I received the same joke by email," Eric says. "Completely unaware of my friend's desires, I sent it to him the same day."

So in spite of some differences, what do these classic cases of meaningful coincidence have in common? Do they each illustrate basic laws that explain why synchronicity happens? Let's take a closer look at this idea.

The Why

Wanting to know the reasons things happen pertaining to us is important to many of us. Maybe most significant here in relation to that is that synchronicity and our ideas about it are absolutely subjective. Because its reality is linked to individual feelings, no one knows what is meaningful or real to anyone else. But by being curious and attentive, paying close attention to our own recurring experiences, we can discover coincidental guidance and events that are genuine, personal and readily available.

The same applies to its mechanics. As a subjective experience of the self, no categorical explanation of how synchronicity works is possible. Sure, we can watch for it, study it – learn its means and ways – give the figure-it-all-out bit our best shot, (as I am doing here). But in the end it can only be proven in private, in the real life labs of its receivers. That being said, my collection of personal coincidental experiences, plus those recounted by numerous others, points to some positively feel good premises. This personal evidence shows:

We live in a wise and responsive Universe that reacts to our thoughts, to our needs and wants. Some invisible force we experience as more powerful and knowing than ourselves supports us through coincidental guidance and helpful circumstances. Whatever happens, it seems we are never alone.

This Universe is regulated and united. Our lives appear to be directed by designs of order and association, their events well arranged and connected. Personal inner and outer experiences are somehow joined, with no division between mental and external happenings. Life, it appears, in all its complexity, is totally interlinked.

Things happen on purpose. Our world is full of mystery; our coincidence of meaning. Magic moves the Universe with sparkle and sense. Bottom line – every happening of our lives is of significance. For instance this nifty example, which closely followed my "Signs! Signs! Signs!" synchronicity, and featured an unexpected twist as sometimes is part of the Universe's magic acts.

A few days have gone by since the earlier experience. I am driving to the grocery store, once again thinking about coincidence. The subject is intriguing as ever, and I'm considering it as the focus of all future research and writing projects. But how wise it that? Just because I'm fascinated by the topic doesn't mean other people are.

So I decide to try the source, to put my question out there, and something more, to ask for a confirmation sign as well. Aloud I say, "Am I on the right track with this? Focusing my work entirely on synchronicity?" Then the experimental addendum, "if I find a penny now, I'll know the answer is yes."

I pull into the parking lot and get out of my car. Though doubtful of finding anything so quickly, I dutifully scan the ground for coins while approaching the store. Nothing. Not unexpected. I mean, the question was raised just a few minutes ago, for heaven's sakes, and this stuff must take some time. Or does it? I surely don't know the answer to that, so just chalk the experiment up as too rushed to be indicative one way or another. And then get on with my shopping.

Once in checkout, a cashier rings up my groceries, tells me the total. I dig into my purse, pull out some cash, hand her the bills. She studies the money for a moment, pauses, then reaches down to a little dish of coins setting on the counter. "Here is a PENNY for you," she says. "So you can have two quarters back in change." Her words take a second to soak in, then the surprise of what has happened washes over me. A penny? This is the requested penny! And along with it my answer. But here's the twist – delivered in a way unlike anything I expected or even imagined. I'm left with a sense of something amazingly limitless.

Lastly, synchronistic experiences seem to show some kind of Universal plan for our balance and blossoming. It's as if a path is in place that when followed leads to our best, most flourishing self. This push towards highest good is expressed in a variety of helpful forms including a most important one – encouragement.

It's May 2013. I'm on my way across town to visit my older parents, thinking about their current circumstances. More precisely, some serious problems that must be solved regarding newly arisen needs. And solved, it turns out, immediately, just as quickly as possible. At the same time, I'm aware that I need to watch my own reactions to these issues, while looking for solutions to them. It would be easy to become pessimistic about the gravity of the whole thing, no help to anyone.

While mulling it all over, the word "focus" pops into my mind. Long a personal favorite, this term has always held a positive connotation for me. Focus, a word that personally refers to concentration on feel-good wants instead of want-nots, resulting in creation of the same. The power of the mind, as I think of it, to conjure up that upon which it is centered. Our part to play in the Universe's magic for sure, when we remember to deliberately choose our point of view.

So with these thoughts in mind I wonder if that's the big answer here. To continue to positively focus, imagine that good outcomes will occur, even though so far nothing has been solved? I like the simple feel of this and hope it's true. Arriving at the complex where my parents live, I head down an inside hallway.

Outside their front door are a couple chairs, a small table, some magazines. A headline on one piece catches my eye with its large and prominent lettering. "FOCUS!" it insists, and I can't help smiling at that. This quick confirmation of my thoughts, this precisely pertinent wording, feels warmly reassuring to me.

Interestingly, the confirmation element of this incident repeats itself in another coincidence a few days later, as if to make sure I really get the message. Once again I am driving (No, I really don't spend most of my time behind the wheel.) and notice the logo of a Ford "Focus" ahead. Because of the recent emphasis on the word, I curiously check out surrounding vehicles and am tickled to see an ad on a bus promising all blue skies instead of gray. This seems to confirm, once again, my ideas about focusing on the good stuff.

The How

With all the buzz in recent years about the "Law of Attraction," most of are somewhat familiar with the term. Law of Attraction, the concept that personal thoughts and feelings attract similar things. More precisely, we attract circumstances and information to us reflecting the essence of them.

Though this idea has been around for a long, long time, with its principles observed and described by philosophical and spiritual writers of both the recent and distant past, it's in the present that it has piqued the interest of scientific minds as well. And possibly been proven in some of their experiments, confirming what many of us already intuitively knew. That our mental focus somehow signals the Universe, resulting in the attraction of things.

The implications of this are downright staggering. If the energy of our thoughts triggers outward replies and circumstances, we literally do, as the popular phrase goes, create our own reality. Furthermore, we are responsible for all its happenings, for the contents of our lives. Mind boggling.

These answers from the Universe can occur with an unlimited number of differences. They always "answer," it seems, what we are "asking" for through our mental concentration. Though the characteristics of each individual response are as varied as our personal thoughts, the forms they take are not. Synchronicities answer our asking through the coincidental appearance of helpful information or events.

This linking of an outer experience with an inner one consistently pertains to our current focus. We send a signal out into the world, it appears, through our strongest thoughts and related feelings. Whatever need or question or desire is presently most important to us serves as the asking, even if we are not consciously aware of it. Whether we are seriously searching for a problem's solution, curiously considering an interesting question, or pleasantly imagining a coveted event, the answers to our asking will come.

This latter part of the equation, the second half of the Law of Attraction's mechanics, may be the most important though often overlooked part. When we mentally ask, synchronicity provides the answers and we benefit. But here's the catch – only if we are actively aware of our environment and watching for its message.

The occurrence of meaningful coincidence often follows a similar sequence of events: the asking; a follow-up intuition; and a synchronicity. In this scenario, our mental focus poses the initial question resulting in inner promptings for us to go somewhere or do something. If we deliberately follow these hunches, coincidentally pertinent information or circumstances will often appear.

Sometimes we may not be outwardly aware of our inner voice's part in this process at all. In these instances our focus is intense and helpful answers quickly seem to materialize. At other times, synchronicities may lead to further insights after their initial occurrences. In any case, it is apparent that our sixth sense as well as our thoughts is a keen player in the phenomena. Consider this unusual dream:

I am attending college, and having trouble finding my

way around the campus. Landmarks of my surroundings such as buildings, roads, and trees keep changing from one instant to the next. I am unhappy about the situation and am shown a book containing explanations. In it one page is titled "Permanent Reality" and a second page, "Flexible Reality." I am shown how reality changes depending on our thoughts and beliefs. To get to where we want to go we must concentrate on it. Outside elements will change continuously, but a pathway to our destination will appear in the middle of it all when we stay focused.

Revisiting the scene of this old dream, I am somewhat surprised at the nifty correlation it holds to current pursuits. The college as a symbol of higher education, the changing landmarks symbolic of the workings of the Law of Attraction. Most interesting is the pathway that appears amongst all the confusion to point the way, as do synchronicities in waking life. Obviously, I've been receiving answers to inward questions about all this stuff a lot longer than I thought!

Another example concerns a fun "test" coincidence that occurred a couple years back. At the time I am experimenting with concrete objectives, in this case focusing on finding an object that is unusual to come across under normal circumstances. My choice? A gold coin. My reasoning? I have never randomly found a gold coin in my life that I can remember, by accident or otherwise.

So I start imagining, a few times a day, finding a gold coin in the street. Nothing too detailed or intense, just casually repeated thinking and picturing of the hoped for event plus feelings of satisfaction about it. A few weeks go by with this routine. Just as I am thinking of dropping the whole attempt as a unsuccessful for whatever reason, it happens. On a busy downtown street, a gleam in the dust catches the light and there it is. A good-sized shiny, glittering, golden coin! A gold coin that on closer inspection proves to be a token of some kind, clearly inscribed "no cash value." Hey, whatever. Maybe specifics or focus are more important in this process than we know.

The Who

So just who is it that experiences meaningful coincidence? A few enlightened individuals? The majority of people? Absolutely everyone? Though it's difficult to share another person's subjective experiences, we can logically assume that if some people have them, most everyone who is able to focus their thoughts probably does as well. An exception might be those who are unable to think clearly, but even then who's to really know? It gets back to the absolutely personal sense of something coincidentally feeling meaningful or not.

If most of us experience synchronicity routinely, why are we sometimes unaware of it? The key word here is unawareness, which probably answers the question. If we are conscious of the existence and personal importance of meaningful coincidence in our lives, we will watch for it and recognize its appearance. If we are unaware and uninterested, we probably won't.

And do we play the same kind of role in these experiences each time they happen? Not hardly. Sometimes we enact the only part, the star, in our own synchronistic productions. Other times our coincidences apparently need a whole cast of supporting characters to play out. Of course, we also assume different roles in the synchronicities of others, from essential key character to bit player, our roles matching the needs of the recipient of the meaningful performance it seems.

A simple case of my part as key player in a synchronicity of my husband's involves a recent shopping trip. We have stopped on the spur of the moment to pick up some produce. He offers to run in while I wait in the car. As Eric climbs out, a thought hits me, and I suggest he take the checkbook along. "In case you are $3 short of cash or something." A few minutes later, he is back with an amused expression on his face. At the checkout the foods' total had come to exactly $3 more than the cash he was carrying. Coincidentally.

Another time our roles are reversed, with Eric playing a key character in my coincidence, and a stranger the essential sidekick. I am writing an article about the allure of old jewelry and considering the word "mystical" for use in the title. Mystical as in something with mysterious secrets or hidden meanings. I wonder, will using the term in an unconventional, non-spiritual way to describe antique jewelry no less, be confusing to readers? I feel stymied and ask Eric his opinion.

He says he doesn't see any conflict with choosing the word, in essence defining the things I write about in my own particular way. Simultaneously as we talk, a TV documentary about something or other is playing in the background. Unexpectedly, the commentator describes someone or something as mystical. This catches my attention. The timely repetition of the somewhat uncommon word feels confirming of my choice of the word, plus its meaning.

The When

Perhaps the bottom line in understanding meaningful coincidence is timing. Synchronicities offer a precisely fit meeting of inner and outer events at just the right moment for us, every time. These happen when we are mentally focused – desiring, deciding, intending, questioning, and at times of turmoil or stressing. The key to their triggering seems to be our level of concentration on personal wants and needs.

These events can concern either major or minor interests, though usually something more than passing thoughts. They normally are about something we are considering, something we are centered on right now. But whether about something serious or light, synchronicities' timing and answers always grab our attention and strike us as uncannily relevant.

An instance of a coincidental quick answer to an everyday question occurred to my son a couple years back during the Christmas holiday. He tells me about it. "I had planned to cook vegetable lasagna from scratch for our family get-together, but had run out of time. While wondering if I could find a tasty pre-made entre version, I flipped on the TV. Immediately an ad for a well-known brand's veggie lasagna began playing, answering my question on the spot." Delicious!

Oftentimes our coincidences occur at transition points in our lives. From there we may be wanting, for instance to add pleasure to our pastimes, our work, our relationships. Or conversely, to eliminate displeasure from the same.

Or maybe we are at a point of general uncertainty, questioning what we should do, which way to go. Or find ourselves with a precise problem in a needful place and looking for help. Chances are that at these important points of potential change we are really focused on our wants and needs, and so coincidental answers will appear.

With that in mind, it is necessary to consider the exceptions to our rule, those events that happen when we aren't concentrating, it seems, on much of anything at all. In these cases there usually is a fleeting flash of insight, sometimes acted upon, sometimes simply observed, followed by a significant coincidence. Of course, it may be a matter of unconscious focus rather than one of which we are much aware. A steady concentration upon a pressing need or strong desire just below our field of awareness as we consciously pay attention to other things.

Or maybe something wiser and more vast than our personalities and individual thoughts is the influential source here – maybe our authentic Higher Self, interrupting and overriding everyday concerns with intuitive guidance about most important things? More on this later....

2

Why Synchronicity? Why Words? Why Now?

Why Synchronicity ?

Mysterious. Secret. Magical. Why do words such as these have the ability to pull us in, play with our minds and mental meanderings? Perhaps because they describe enchantment – that awe-inspiring charmer with its puzzling power to make things happen, to influence events. Based on current cultural expressions, we crave that sense of wonder.

In the "new age," many of us are dissatisfied with general scientific theories of a mechanized Universe. Our cultures reflect a steadily growing fascination with anything cryptic and unexplained. We long for inner contentment and lasting joy, with bits of bewitchment thrown in. We long to be part of a world of hidden magic and in communication with the magician.

Throughout recorded history, belief in a connected Universe has been common. In many cultures the creative force has been seen to communicate with us through signs and other symbols. This link to something wiser and wittier than ourselves felt magnificent and mysterious then. And it still does.

September 2012, Salem: It's evening, and I'm dreaming of a green and grassy park, luminous on a sunlit day. Within the scene I am lying on a gently rising hill, contemplating cottony clouds above. Suddenly, in the middle of my reverie – *kerplunk* – something falls softly but directly onto my face. I jump up, startled, glance all around. Finding nothing out of the ordinary, I laugh aloud at the jest, the joke just played on me. And I take a close look at what fell from the sky.

It's a flower, a freshly picked, pristine rose. A perfectly petaled rich golden, fragrant, stemless rose. I am impressed! Still, I speculate, well, this could just be a coincidence. Then sensing the absurdity of that idea I reconsider, and say aloud, "No, it's not! It is a sign. A gift from above!" Then I wake up.

Later, when reflecting on the dream's message, I think first of my mixed feeling toward roses. In particular, the variation between their sweet smelling, magnificent flowers and their nondescript leaves and thorns. In comparison, my dream rose was just right, beautiful and stemless of a warm shade that always reminds me of sunshine and happy things.

The dream message seems obvious. The Universe is both generous and lighthearted, plus well aware of our likings. And as comically pointed out, it communicates through signs. Even if it has to smack us between the eyes with them to get our attention!

Similarly, my affinity for this subject of synchronicity was communicated by an episode of the same. A meaningful incident that like the previous dream, left no doubt as to its message. For as long as I can remember, I have always loved doing research, of searching for and ferreting out valuable information. The continual offerings of newness and variety, plus unexpected surprises are ever exciting to me.

I especially enjoy the adventure of following novel ideas and intuitive insights to new discoveries about "mind stuff" – unrecognized or undeveloped mental abilities we all may have. So as my awareness of this subject grew, my interest and the coincidences did too, the following one a pleasant endorsement of my focus.

March 2011, Salem: I've been wondering lately if synchronicity is the one subject I need to concentrate on in research to be happiest in my work. I begin a new novel with the question percolating in the back of my mind. Within a few pages, a character states that there are no coincidences, that everyone is a link. I sense the occurrence of this comment as a clear response that yes, this is the subject most satisfactory for me.

Besides reaffirming the rightness of my keen interest, the message feels good for another reason, too. As a phenomena who's understanding can increase meaningfulness and joy, synchronicity holds inherent life-changing potential. Any knowledge I might uncover towards self-discovery or personal growth may be of worth to us all.

Why Words?
Words are our messengers. Though images, objects, sounds

and other non-literary symbols may be also, it's to words we typically turn when we want to communicate. As does the Universe. Coincidences involving some kind of words, either written or spoken or both, are one of the most common ways the cosmos provides us with answers— answers that we find significant AND personally precise.

Observations of my experiences, and those of others shared with me over the years, lead me to believe that written or spoken word synchronicities tend to occur to people depending by how they think and take in information. How a person prefers to perceive the world and reflect on it determines which type of coincidence each one is likely to have.

Of course, this is a theory based on subjective experiences, knowledge gained from real life by contact with facts and events. Facts and events that have happened in the everyday world. This may be the best (or only) way coincidence can be studied. As synchronicities concern links occurring within the worlds of private lives, it's to these personal stories, and particularly the words of their messages, that we must turn.

Paying attention to the coincidental tales of others can be fun and enlightening, especially what they experience in relation to their intellectual style. But where we really might gain is determining our own favored way of thinking and perceiving.

This may lead to an exciting and helpful self-discovery, what special type of synchronicity we are likely to experience. We'll delve into this later.

Why Now?

June 2011, Salem: I'm walking from my parking spot to the library to work. As I move along, noticing the various sights of the neighborhood, a decorative paper laying on the sidewalk catches my attention. So I stop and take a closer look. It's a playing card, a black on white ace of spades. It's clean and crisp with an elaborate embellished design. And strangely enough, looks like it has just that moment been dropped onto the ground.

Immediately, memories come up of other pieces of found paper I have come across in the past, including several other ace of spades cards. And then other images of the symbol that seem to pop up here and there for me. The whole thing feels a little odd, like *something* may be astir. So I determine to satisfy my curiosity with a little digging.

A bit later, I look at a book on cartomancy, or divination with common playing cards. In *The Cards of Your Destiny: Look Into Your Past, Present, and Future Using the Ancient and Original Science of Card Reading,* author Robert Camp teaches a method of self-discovery and prediction.

Scanning the book, I note that in its system a person's birthday card is determined, which then plays a role in yearly spreads. There is a detailed section on interpretation, meanings for each card in the deck. Since that is what I am most curious about, historical meanings assigned to the ace of spades, I read that first.

The author goes into much detail about the symbolism of the card. He explains its meanings, its history, its lore. Unfortunately, I am not able to reach him later to be able to share his ideas here. But then, this story is not over.

I find the material on the ace of spades utterly fascinating. Though cartomancy is new to me, and I have not looked into it enough to personally validate or invalidate its concepts, I resonate with the card's profile. Its symbol's meaning uncannily concerns what I find most intriguing. And that is odd.

So I decide to explore the system a bit further by looking up my birthday card, which is determined by my birth date. And there it is again – listed as the one card in the deck most reflective of the real me – the ace of spades!

Later in the evening, I am reviewing my research notes for the day. I re-read this material on card reading, and get an urge to play with a deck. And do exactly what I wonder? I'm not at all sure. But I do, and sit there shuffling it over and over for awhile. Then randomly I draw a card and flip it over. It's the ace of spades.

It feels so eerie that I'm compelled to repeat the maneuver, and when I do another spade comes up, this time a seven. So I shuffle once more and again it appears – the ace. Quickly I put the cards away.

It seems my work's focus is being observed. I began my research into synchronicity at the beginning of the year. Sometime in the middle of it, an interest in a completely different topic arose, and I considered working on that instead of the first. After being briefly undecided, I returned to my investigation of coincidence, then promptly found the ace.

At the beginning of 2012, I start writing a second book.

Its background research is fun, and I am able to comfortably combine the two projects for awhile. Then the inner either or debate starts up and I decide once more to work exclusively with coincidence.

The new year of 2013 begins, and I'm happily involved in writing and research for this book when family needs pull me away. After one particularly grueling week, I'm riding home from helping with an appointment in Portland. I have a quick regret about my writing, or rather the lack of time for it lately. I mentally question, *Is synchronicity really important for me to study? Or just an extremely interesting topic?*

At that moment, I look out the window and see a small sign by the side of the road. It sports an arrow pointing left to something or other unseen around the corner. And the name of whatever, *The Ace of Spades.* I try to see what's being named, but we are in a hurry, and as we speed by I am left with just the coincidence and its words. But for now that's quite enough.

Later, I am writing up these stories of the ace. As I write, it's fun to remember their surprising occurrence and stimulating effect, as if a higher force was both orchestrating it all and prompting my participation. I want to know more.

In *The Cards of Your Destiny*, Robert Camp references an antiquarian text about the cartomancy system. It was published by a gentleman named Olney Richmond back in 1893. Naturally, this piques my interest. Because of its age, I find that the book now belongs to the United States public domain. I download the entire thing from an archives site on the internet and start reading.

The title is enlightening in itself as to the comprehensiveness of what's to come, and by whom. Its detailed summary reads: *"The Mystic Test Book or the Magic of the Cards: Giving the Mystic Meaning of those Wonderful and Ancient Emblems in their Relationship to the Heavenly Bodies, Under all Conditions; With Rules and Processes for Reading or Delineating the Emblems."*

It continues, "Written and Compiled Under the Authority of the Mystic Brotherhood. By Olney H. Richmond. Grand Master of the Inner Temple of Ancient Order of the Magi."

Olney's dedication then reads in part, "For those who have an affinity for the good, the pure and the true, as well as the spiritual advancement and development which enable them to comprehend the mysteries of the infinite and majestic Universe."

I consider the author's signature as "Grand Master" of a mystery group he claims had been directed since ancient times to guard the secrets of the cards. Apparently, the time of publication was right for their disclosure. Near the end of the book, he expands on this, saying in part, "This Order is a true Secret Order in the fullest sense of the word....But the *Religion of the Stars*, which is the religion of the Order is *not secret.*"

He discusses those ancient Magi, said to have held the original meanings of the cards, as understanding the deeper hidden principle underlying symbolism. That "there is a spirit force back of everything that exists..." and "a psychic recognition of the hidden things in nature." And regarding chance he explains, "But it is now known that no such thing exists as chance, at least in the regard to the majority of things, and we know that nothing comes by chance."

Pretty quickly I find discussion of some familiar topics. Such as correspondence of the 52 cards in a deck with weeks in a year, 12 court cards with the months, and 13 cards of each suit with the sun plus the dozen zodiacal signs. The four suits are likewise said to represent nature's four seasons.

And here's where things get particularly pertinent. I hone in as Olney explores the symbolism of the suits, saying that the fourth quarter of the Zodiac – or winter – is represented by the spade or acorn. He explains, "By a strange and yet natural transformation, the acorn, which represented the death and burial of the physical form was changed among some nations to the spade which represented the same thing.

"But the acorn, when planted in the soil, sends forth a life principle which becomes a new tree in time. ...the spade being an instrument of labor, it becomes a symbol of labor and death."

Interesting. So the suit of spades seems to have evolved into standing for work, endings *and* renewal. Like all symbols, its meanings may apply to both outer and inner things as well. And what about the ace? Are its associations the same, or more involved than those of its suit? We have all probably noticed how the card looks different than all others in a deck. The symbol is often much larger and more richly decorated. Sometimes there is a manufacturer's name on the card, too. What does the author of this old and unusual book have to say about the ace of spades?

He calls it by different names throughout the text – the "Secret emblem," the "Magi card," the "Secret Magi emblem," and speaks of "The ace of spades, the *secret emblem,* representative of the *secret order*...illustrating the cards first meaning. At the time *The Mystic Test Book* was published, the symbol stood not only for secret knowledge, but occult societies as well. The ace of spades was *the* symbol of the Order of the Magi and its secret studies of the cards.

The word "secret" here is key. Olney describes the ace of spades as the secret and mystic card, indicative of a person with a mystic disposition and love of secret, unusual information. Depending on its location in divinatory spreads, the card also can symbolize secret knowledge or com-munications. Or occult psychic power. Or secret wishes or letter or plans, and more. You get the picture.

Later, I think about the whole play of events. In particular, the puzzling pull of the symbol, and my unexplained drive to learn about it. There had been a sense of urgency, like something important was trying to get through, trying to communicate through the symbolism of the ace. Then there was the matter of the books. Why had I been drawn to study these particular titles when others, with other symbol definitions may have been around? Were these events to guide my work and illuminate my path?

I can't help but think so. How the meanings in these books both affected and surprised me. How they spoke of my passions and what I love to do. It seems the Universe dealt me a "birthday card," that as Olney said, "has a part to play all through life." A card whose meanings and presence seems impossible to ignore. And there lies the significance.

3

The Beauty & Benefits of Meaningful Coincidence

January 2015, Salem: My niece Alisha emails me to share this entertaining story. "I was on my walking break at work today. At the start of my walk I told my best bud co-worker that I needed to look up a diet for arthritis because my finger joints have really been aching. That was the end of that topic. We walked on, talking of other things.

"Halfway through our mile, we were crossing the street. On the other side there was an older homeless appearing gentleman. He stopped us and said, "Excuse my attitude, but here is a tip. If you eat a stalk of celery every day your joints won't ache. I like mine with peanut butter.'" Alisha sums up her feelings on this most curious incident, "I personally consider it one of God's gifts in the coincidence category!"

Later, I think about the different threads of life that had to twine together to create this helpful event for Alisha. It seems that a stranger to both my niece and her friend had a possible answer to her question. But here's the catch – they never would have heard it if he hadn't stopped them in the street.

And then there was the matter of timing. If the two women hadn't happened to cross the street at the precise time the guy was approaching from the other side, there would have been no coincidental meeting. And accordingly, no beneficial answer.

It becomes apparent pretty quickly that a huge benefit of synchronicity is its response to questions. When we pay attention to the coincidences of our lives, we receive answers. Knowing that we have a ready source of information available to answer both light and serious inquiries about anything and everything feels quite simply super – IF we are personally able to let go and trust the knowingness of our source.

In essence, all benefits of coincidence are answers. In response to our questions about life, the serene sense of security we may experience when we realize we are never alone. Through the significance of these happenings we come to know we are somehow connected to everything, and everyone, including something far greater and wiser.

And in response to questions about ourselves, more happiness and fulfillment. Through the meaningful messages of coincidence we learn to become our best selves, by pursuing the passions of our true selves. Synchronistic events seem to prove we play a major part in an interconnected Universe when we follow our quirks.

So beyond these effects of personal meaning and satisfaction, what are the benefits of the phenomena? The "answers" arrive in a myriad of good feeling forms, probably an infinite number, considering the origin. Here are some biggies – major types of coincidental benefits I have seen or experienced.

Answers to Questions

Even if we view all synchronicities as answers of some type or other, we can observe this benefit specifically when aware of personal inquiries. If we remember instances of the past, and are alert to our current questions, we will recognize coincidental answers.

These responses don't discriminate by seriousness. They seem to come in answer to whatever question we think of persistently, whatever matters to us. Apparently, to the Universe, any question we firmly entertain is important and deserves an answer. Whether about something light, curious, or life-changing, it appears our questions are always answered synchronistically.

Solutions to Problems

Similarly, when our asking involves a problem, the answer is a solution. We receive guidance through a meaningful coincidence that addresses the dilemma. It doesn't seem to matter if the topic of concern is of major importance or is inconsequential. Solutions are provided through helpful messages or consequences.

My friend Deidre shares, "Daniel and I were visiting our daughter in New Mexico. While there, we ran short of silverware for meals so picked up an extra set. It turned out that each of the new utensils had a sticky label almost impossible to remove." Deidre continues, "I worked on the clean-up job while Sara ran to town to do some errands. Later, when she returned, Sara also brought me some nail polish pads, as I had run out of them the day before.

Coincidentally, the acetone of the pads was exactly what was needed to remove the silverware labels' gunk. "

Love & Caring

One of the most comforting benefits of synchronicity is loving concern. The cosmos cares about us personally, and is watchful of our endeavors. This affection for the individual is seen to encompass the total person. Coincidental messages and circumstances of love and caring relate to both our physical and mental selves.

Whatever is going on in our lives, it is comforting to be reminded that the Universe is both loving and supportive. We receive its care and concern in the form of synchronistic events. When we find meaning in these happenings we are reassured, and feel confident that we are really never alone.

December 2011, Salem: It's the end of the winter, a cold, damp and dreary day. I'm getting ready to attend an event I'd really rather not, for a variety of reasons. I feel obligated to go, however. So while dressing, I make an effort to let my feelings of discomfort subside.

I'm unsure what to wear to the event, which will be held outdoors – I want to stay both warm and comfortable. So I consider my choices carefully, then pull a wool blazer from the closet. The jacket is pretty, a vivid bright blue. I have only worn it once or twice before, because of its weight. But today it seems just right. As I start to slip on the blazer, the name on its label jumps out at me. "Nanci-Jennifer" it proudly reads. Instantly I get goose bumps.

This feels obviously significant, right now, somehow. I'm just not sure how. I have a dear friend, Nancy, who I plan to see tomorrow. Could this sign with our two names refer to that get-together? I feel unsure of the meaning of the message, but certain that there is one – when I can decipher it. Meanwhile there's a comfy sense of rightness about wearing the jacket.

A few months go by, and once again I am standing at the closet, checking out my clothes. I notice the blazer and the whole past scenario of the uncomfortable event and next day's visit with my friend mentally replays. I think about Nancy. How she is the best sort of friend a person can have – soft-hearted, fun and kind – how she is ever ready to listen and lend her help, however it is needed.

In a flash, I understand the meaning of the Nanci-Jennifer coincidence as a caring reminder. A reminder of this special friendship and its supportive role in stressful times. And beyond this, the confirmation of Universal intelligence that cares about my personal concerns!

Encouragement & Inspiration

The benefit that I have noticed most in my personal experiences of synchronicity is encouragement. Instances of some kind of cosmic support are often evident when I pay attention. It's as if the Universe notices when we need a lift and arranges coincidences to provide it. Messages that encourage us arrive in ways that seem accidental, yet feel meaningful. And in these instances we are left feeling better – inspired really – to start or continue some personal pursuit.

Sometimes these instances concern things that are very important to us, and we experience big coincidences. Messages or events coinciding in an impressively significant way that are clearly supportive. And sometimes they are about the little things of life like minor decisions and goals. It's Universal support that feels subtle yet encouraging. In either case, we are provided with inspiration in an uncanny synchronistic way and enlivened along our path.

Confirmation & Direction

August 2013, Salem: I'm browsing, somewhat detachedly, in a local craft supply store. After hearing of a friend's ailment, a question is on my mind. Can a person ensure her or his own good health? Is this even possible to do? I approach the store's scrapbooking section, filled with all types of decorative papers. The spectrum of colors and patterns is enticing, and I rummage through remnant stacks of assorted prints. One piece, decorated with an interesting thought catches my eye. "The perfect way to know what's ahead? Create it!"

I have, of course, heard different versions of this idea before. But right now it has a answering feel about it. Could it be a message in response to my question? I have not been actively seeking an answer – consciously anyway. But the question has been repeating in my mind. I resume my browsing, moving on to another aisle. An exhibit of DIY calendars displays an advertising sign above. "Make Your Own Calendar!" it exclaims. I feel a little thrill recognizing another symbolic way.

A few days later something reminds me again of this idea of predicting your own future, your good health in this case, by creating it. Just what's the best way to do that I wonder? With all the information and opinions out there, much of it conflicting, the whole thing can be confusing. Not to mention complicated. A simple and certain route to continual well-being would be great.

I'm thinking about this while pulling into a shopping center parking lot. I see a store called "Habits." Of course, this is the answer! Our personal habits, those mental and physical actions that we repeat over and over, are sure to have some kind of consequence. The trick is to create positive ones, doing things we intuitively know are good for us, over and over and over.

I receive another confirmation of these concepts shortly thereafter, while considering my friend's situation. I think about persistence and habits and creating good health. Alongside the road a series of small signs boasts of benefits for some business in the area. "Good Future!" one proclaims, speaking on one level about local jobs. And on another reminding me coincidentally of the overall consequence of these actions. Thank you, Universe!

When it comes to confirmation of our choices, the Universe can be reassuring. Through synchronicity, validating our choices by meaningful events. These coincidental messages may verify or clarify our present position or our current course. Reaffirm that we are moving the right way

– are on track. Or conversely that we are not, and heading in the wrong direction.

Things seem to run smoothly when confirming coincidences are happening. We feel reassured that we have made a right decision or that things will work out. Or we may receive help for making the choice that's correct for us in the first place.

Directional coincidences also can work in the opposite way. Instead of "GO" signs, we may experience synchronistic events that indicate "STOP." We can't seem to reach a goal because of slow-downs. Or get going at all because of blocks. Whichever their message, synchronicities of confirmation or direction help us find our best path and stay on it.

Warnings

Mid-winter, Salem: It's afternoon, and I'm working at the library. My time is limited today, so I am in a bit of a hurry to locate some important reference materials. Among the stacks I spot a credit card dropped on the floor. Probably hurrying like me, I think to myself about the owner's carelessness. Then pick up the card and head to checkout to turn it in.

Just around the corner something else has been dropped on the floor. It turns out to be a bunch of five or six little pencils, of the type set out for use by the computers. Again I think of rushing and carelessness. Suddenly a thought comes to mind – have I lost anything? I have certainly been hurrying and scurrying around. I check out the stack of books I am carrying and see that yes, I have left a couple essential titles somewhere in the library! I begin looking for the forgotten books, retracing MY careless steps.

What can be better than having a personal security system provided by the cosmos? It seems when we pay attention to messages of caution provided by coincidence, it's like receiving a tap on the shoulder from the Universe. Apparently, these warnings can be about matters of any size – both the big and little stuff of life – whatever our current focus concerns. And usually arrive via words. Sometimes the written or spoken messages involve images too.

Take my synchronicity described here. The company name on the credit card, seen in an obviously out of place location, triggered thoughts of misplaced things. Plus ideas of careless rushing. The pencils laying on the floor somehow reinforced the image, leading to concerns about my own hurrying.

Maybe the hardest part of recognizing these warnings is that they can be subtle, and concerned with small matters. As opposed to dramatically relevant cautions about serious things. But what a help for us to notice the coincidences about our everyday affairs as well.

Humor & Fun

Afternoon, Salem: Eric and I are driving along, discussing our latest quest. We have been unsuccessfully searching for a DVD version of an old movie starring Walter Matthau. The

1970 comedy, "A New Leaf," also features Elaine May. The story of the couple and their mishaps is hilarious and Eric and I really want to own the film. But it seems to be available only in VCR, and we haven't been able to find a copy here.

We chat about the places we have already checked, movie rental and general discount stores, local thrift stores, antique shops, and a number of yard sales. Still the film is elusive, and the whole thing is starting to bug me. I complain a little about the situation, then look out the window to see a message, written just for me.

"Relief from the Leaf!" a billboard promises in an ad for a gutter guard system. I am instantly amused and feel like something or someone more worldly is saying, "Hey, lighten up. This is no big deal. You will find that old movie soon enough!" And gently poking fun at me for being annoyed at the same time.

We do find the film shortly, or rather Eric does. And by a coincidence as well. While walking on an errand he is forced to detour around some construction. A small, previously unknown shop with "Movies" is spotted. And as you might guess, just happens to have a single copy of the old movie. Relief from the leaf indeed!

One of the most exciting benefits of synchronicity is its gift of amusement. Coincidental events point the way to our enjoyment of humor and fun. It's as if the creative force wants us to indulge in everything that is personally possible and makes us happy. Plus those things that make us smile and laugh. If we can learn to recognize the clues, the symbols and events offered for our guidance, and understand their messages, we are on our way to more pleasure and play.

Sometimes these synchronistic words lead us to a means of being able to make favorite pastimes major parts of our lives. Sometimes they help us determine which things are most enjoyable in the first place. And sometimes they guide us to previously unexpected pursuits we discover we love.

It seems that humor is often an essential part of significant coincidence. Synchronicities convey comical messages through the meanings of their words. These meanings may be literal – based on the sense of the actual words, or symbolic – derived from our personal associations to them. Either way they feel relevant, playful, and sometimes downright funny.

It's as if the Universe is amused by our shenanigans and wants to share the good-hearted feelings or remind us of the lighter side of life that always present. In any case, the messages are humorous and expressed through meanings or the play of words and leave us smiling and entertained.

Wisdom & Spiritual Lessons

Some experiences of synchronicity offer us the gifts of insight and instruction. Wisdom and spiritual truths are communicated through significant words. It seems that the purpose of these coincidences is to reassure us that higher forces exist. And that everyone and everything is connected.

We often trigger these answers with our questions about the world, consciously or otherwise. And the Universe responds. With coincidental messages of enlightenment about the interconnected cosmos and our important roles within it. The message is that each and every one of our individual lives is important in the big picture.

Sometimes synchronicities of this type appear to happen without our prior questioning at all. Communications occur coincidentally with the sole purpose, it seems, of awakening us to our link with everything else. We may experience an inner knowing of the reality of something greater than ourselves and feel a comforting reassurance that we are never alone.

The coincidental messages can be transformative – our priorities may shift and change. What we desire most in our lives may suddenly and completely change. The receipt of Universal truths often uproots things one way or another, in our inner or outer worlds. Our thoughts, attitudes and overall way of seeing may simply (or painfully) change. Whatever the outcome, however, "accidental" messages of spiritual wisdom are often our most prized experiences.

Creative Materialization

Eric retells me this favorite tale. "It was spring 1972, and I was living in Los Angeles. I was single at the time and had fallen in love with a bicycle. It was a Fuji Finest, a lightweight ten-speed, graceful and fast. Often I would just sit and study the model pictured on the front of a bicycle buyers' guide. I really admired the good lines of the deep blue and chrome beauty. And wanted it badly. But the price was just too much.

"Then a letter came one day from my mother. She was a recreational gambler and had recently done well at the races. I was delighted to discover that, seemingly out of the blue, she had enclosed a check for the exact price of the Fuji!"

The helpful coincidence became a cluster. Though he remained in the area after college, Eric had become increasingly uncomfortable with L.A. The sprawling city's size and air quality just didn't jive with his values.

He began taking longer and longer rides on the bike for relaxation and fun. He rode it to work, to friends' houses, to the beach. And then one day the thought came – I could just get on my bike and ride out of here into the sunset – for good! And so he did just that, after quitting his job and selling his car, with the Fuji providing the means.

North in Oregon, Eric settled into the western valley town of Albany for the winter. He had already ridden more than 1,500 miles to Montana and back. In the spring, he planned to move further west to Hawaii – until some events happened to occur.

Living in the same town, I went out for the evening. A college deal proved dull, so I headed to a dancehall restaurant with friends. Meanwhile, across town, Eric chatted with a guy while playing pool and accompanied him to the same place for the very first time. We met when the music started, and our timing coincided. And both felt the meaning of the eventful night.

Besides guidance, materialization is the other major type of synchronicity. The cosmos brings things into being through the occurrence of meaningful coincidence. These usually are things we really want or need and things we really are focusing upon, things we are picturing, thinking, and talking about.

As in this example, when Eric concentrated on the bicycle and its price over and over. He imagined himself riding it along with experiencing how good that would feel. This focus was apparently the trigger to the chance response, his mother's unexpected gift.

Circumstances can even result from concentration on unwanted stuff. Synchronistic events are that result. It appears the Universe interprets our interest centers as requests. And orchestrates happenings. Good focus – or not – what a wonderful benefit to understand! How to be part of making our own magic from the gift of coincidence.

4

Types of Synchronicity

December 2012, Salem: It's nearly Christmas and Eric and I are discussing the holidays. In the background on the radio, a melodious guitarist plays sweetly. "This isn't a gift idea," he says, "but I would really like to own a guitar." He goes on to reminisce about an instrument he once owned many years before. "Maybe teach myself to play. It would be so fun to do jazz and blues – recognizably," he jokes. We laugh and move on to other topics.

A couple weeks go by. One evening our son Jason calls to visit. He talks about work, the unpredictability of his job in property management. "It can be a real mess when people vacate quickly," he explains. "You'd be surprised at the things I have to dispose of."

"Like what?" Eric asks.

"Like several big boxes of sheet music I have right now," Jason says. "Oh, and the guitar that goes with them. I like to find homes for these things where they are appreciated." Needless to say, this was one discarded item that received just that on Christmas Eve. When Eric received a very special gift – his favorite!

Coincidence is clever. From an unlimited palate of possibilities it dishes up our choices. Through a savory selection of "chance" events, it offers what we want, in the form of significant events, in the form of significant words, concocting its mixture of meaningful happenings for our tastes alone.

Materializations and messages seem to be the two major forms of synchronicity. The main ways coincidence operates and comes into our lives. Within these forms, however, the phenomena expresses itself in a boundless assortment of chance incidents, each one utterly unique.

This incredible medley of happenchance events is truly the spice of it all. Adding flavor and relish to everyday life through variety of circumstance and words. With a sprinkle of meaningful mystery, and a dash of piquant surprise, the Universe serves up some delicious experiences, creation and wisdom-wise.

Words play an important part in most synchronicities. Whether in the form of messages from Universal intelligence, or materializations by the same, they usually involve words. The creation of things in response to our needs often includes information. And coincidental messages of all types usually arrive through words. Even the less common guidance conveyed through other symbols may include them as well.

So it is the language of coincidence to which we must turn when investigating its types. The use of language that plays a part in almost every instance. Of course, any listing of varieties of the phenomena is purely subjective, as the Universe holds the ultimate skill in creating ever new scenarios, and combining – and overlapping – synchronistic "types" at will.

Just the same, here are some variables that are often seen in coincidence. With a look at the language that differs in each. Written words, or spoken words, or messages of both. When it comes to types of the phenomena, variety abounds.

Solitary or Together

Some incidents of meaningful coincidence involve only one person. The information provided, a solution, confirmation etc., is meant for our eyes or ears alone. No one else is physically involved. In these cases we happen upon pertinent information by ourselves, through the written or spoken word coincidentally.

With the first, our message can come through a myriad of different kinds of written materials – a book, an advertisement, a paper scrap – whatever. And when we happen upon it we KNOW that this is our answer. Of course, any writing outside of our own originates with someone else, conveying their ideas, thoughts, or dreams. But in these instances we receive significant feeling guidance without direct contact with others.

October 2013, Salem: A local post office where we receive our mail may be closing. We consider other locations, then decide to buy into a unit of locked boxes on our street. Eric makes the arrangements, then selects one of the empty boxes at random. He tries out the new key and finds that our address has already been written in that particular box. Good choice!, the coincidence seems to say.

With solitary types of synchronicity involving the spoken word, we again are the sole recipient of a message. Other people – friends, acquaintances, or strangers serve as instruments to bring the needed information to us. We may have a conversation about our particular topic of concern, or be talking to others about something completely different. Either way, the coincidental response to our interest comes through what the other party says.

Or we may overhear the conversation of people unknown to us, or one of their passing remarks, that happens to include pertinent facts. Again, the others involved are part of the incident for our benefit, to bring us its message.

Together types of synchronicities involve the needs of several individuals. For instance, a couple of people may be focused on the same subject, experience the same event, and interpret it the same way. Just as likely, several people coincidentally brought together will have different needs. The event plays out as their concerns somehow coincide and are individually answered. Responses may be through written or spoken words, circumstances, or a combination of these.

October 2013, Santa Rosa CA: Eric and I are vacationing in the well known warm and picturesque wine community, considering it for a future home. Though the countryside looks quite different than Salem, the city itself doesn't. I remark on this resemblance while we are driving around town. "Like that?" Eric asks, pointing at the next street sign we pass. "Salem Avenue" it reads, seemingly in agreement!

Major or Minor Role

A second common variable of coincidence concerns character parts. In meaningful events with others we take on roles of different dimensions. As the receiver of our own experiences, we naturally play the lead, with others acting out communicative parts of major or minor size. The Universe sets the stage, it seems, with the perfect kinds of characters – even if they aren't aware of it.

Important information can come through anyone involved in our meaningful events, and then, of course, vice versa, through us in theirs. What is significant here is that everyone who pays a role in a synchronicity is essential – even if they aren't aware of their role.

Simple or Complex

Meaningful coincidences can be simple or they can be complex, sometimes exceedingly so. Taking a second look at the previously related story of Eric, his bicycle, and our happenchance meeting, it's easy to see how intricate these events can be. Thankfully, we are not the ones who have to arrange their patterns. With the help of the Universe, complicated puzzles of coincidental words and events gently lead us to the solutions we seek.

For instance, Eric's original plan was to leave L.A. and ride north to the town of Marina in central California. Here, at his sister's home, he would pedal his way to Oregon, and to a long time friend's home near Albany. After a short visit, he planned to ride to the home of other close friends in Montana, again for a visit of just a few days. Finally, he hoped to leave Montana, bicycle across the northern United States to the East Coast then south to Florida.

Early on, things did not work out as planned. A knee injury the first day out resulted in a longer visit with his sister, who happened to be grappling with a personal situation she was eager to discuss. Eric offered some options that were welcomed. In addition, to make his long ride a little less strenuous, he spent some time and money installing new bicycle gears. So his planned visit of a couple days turned into ten or so.

The second stopover of his trip turned out as long. Eric's Oregonian friend was a military buddy, and the two hadn't seen each other for awhile, so their visit was fun and restful. Spending more time together just felt right.

Eric's third stop in Montana turned out similarly – a longer than planned visit with friends, plus an offer of somewhere to stay. But dwindling funds and the approaching winter cold altered his plans. Things that just happened to occur changed his course and he headed back to Oregon.

Occurrences such as these amaze us with their intricacy. The twists and turns leading up to the events are complex and involved, for in reality, the synchronicities must begin at some earlier time for their disparate elements to come together so beautifully.

Individuals' needs somehow connect, each one heard

and met. Peoples' desires interlock, helping to realize each other. It's as if the perfect path to what we want (for Eric, a new home, and for both of us, a new relationship), leads best when shared with another.

Take this example. At what point did the coincidences that resulted in our meeting really begin for Eric? When he was held up at his sister's at the beginning of his trip? When he became dissatisfied with Los Angeles? Received the surprise check from his mom? Or did it begin far earlier – at the moment he fell in love with the Fuji – and decided he wanted it?

And what about his partners in the events, his sister for example. Had she only recently focused on wanting someone close to talk to about her circumstances? Or had this been a desire of hers for some time? If so, it seems for things to click the timing had to be right for both of them, to synchronize their needs while protecting their free wills.

Whenever and wherever the process begins, there will be clues along the way, written or spoken words that nudge towards steps to take each day. Because with these complex events things may be quite involved, and getting there take some time. But what a great gift from the cosmos to us when we follow flow to it.

In comparison to this, synchronicity is sometimes exceedingly simple – uncomplicated, right-on responses to our inner thoughts and needs. In these instances, little effort seems needed on our part, as what we want shows up quickly and coincidentally in our lives.

It may be that the requested information, object or

experience is merely easier to arrange in the Universal orchestra of events. Harmonizing the elements is fast and smooth. Or it may be a result of something completely different – our awareness. When we follow our intuitions and pay attention to our surroundings, communicating with us through coincidence may be simpler.

November 2013, Salem: Eric, the conjuring king of shopping, tells me that he is looking for a particular style of cold weather mask for bicycling, priced at no more than $5. He gets an urge to try a particular sporting goods store and finds other styles priced much higher. Then he spots a single mask, laying on the floor, and it's exactly what he wants. It just happens to cost $5.

A few days later, a similar scenario occurs to me, this time involving words. I have already bought my sister's Christmas presents for the holiday, when she mentions that she would love to receive a new flannel shirt. I tell Eric that if I come across a new one at a thrift store for $5 or so, I will add it to her other gifts. Later, we browse a couple of stores where I find nothing. Eric suggests a third that doesn't sound promising to me. I decide to consider this idea as a possible synchronistic message arriving through my husband. We head for the store. Once there, I find a pretty, new ladies flannel shirt priced at $10. But since it is half price day, I end up paying only $5, coincidentally.

Big or Small
Closely related to the variable of complexity is that of

importance. Synchronicity varies from the momentous to the commonplace. Some coincidences are really big. Messages or circumstances pertaining to deeply meaningful personal themes. Others are smaller – significant feeling communications or events about non-essentials. Whether about the serious or the slight, however, observation shows us that the Universe treats the subject matter of our focus with equal concern.

It often appears that coincidences concerned with matters of paramount importance are also complex, as if the seriously big stuff is harder to arrange. And that synchronicities about lighter, more common issues are usually simple. This may be the case with human endeavors but not necessarily the Universal. Personally speaking, anyway, I've found the opposite to sometimes be true. When I pay attention and follow coincidental clues, simple wording sometimes provides deep insights.

We do have many instances of simple synchronicities, of course, which are about the commonplace, coincidental guidance and arrangements that help us flow through everyday concerns. These episodes seem to arise and conclude quickly when we notice them and are alert to their messages.

November 2013, Salem: Eric and I decide to try a phone service device with a low monthly cost to replace our landline. We buy it and attempt to register and activate the system online. For some reason, our credit card, which is carrying no balance, is not accepted for billing purposes.

Several calls to the phone service and the card company do not resolve the problem.

We are told to go ahead and hook up the device – that the billing issue will be resolved later. We do and try a test call. Very quickly, the signal is lost and the call disconnects. We check our Internet connection, which is fine, then try another call. It immediately disconnects like the first time. Now we feel uncomfortable with the entire situation. Something about it – the selection, the timing, whatever – just isn't right. We both sense "STOP" signs in the deal and decide to cancel the whole thing.

Single or Cluster

Synchronicities can occur as solitary events or as groups. Meaningful coincidence varies by number. Sometimes a single message or circumstance from the Universe answers our needs, and that is the end of it. Other times, it seems to take a cluster of communications to make sure we get the point. Or to arrange things – orchestrate our desires.

Clusters can also occur as a bunch of coincidences concerning different aspects of the same subject. When we are focused on an important goal, it sometimes takes numerous steps and corrections to get what we want. Higher intelligence helps by providing guidance, information, and materializations as needed. The following group of happenchance events occurred over a few days of busy and concentrated activity.

January 2013, Corvallis OR: My sister Gayle and I are

planning a large anniversary party for our parents. She is busy making all the decorations at her home in Corvallis, to be later transported the hour's drive to Salem. Some items are big and bulky, and we are relying on her minivan for this. Suddenly, something mechanical breaks down and the vehicle won't run. Though the event is still a few days away, the van is needed now to pick up some rental props. We are in a bind.

Gayle's husband remembers a mechanic who just happens to live nearby He checks with the guy who luckily has the time, right now, to take a look at the van. He does and quickly discovers the defective part. Then, rummaging through his supplies finds, coincidentally, a used sample of the uncommon part. It is installed immediately and we are back in business.

The next day, Gayle and I are working on the refreshments. Our most pressing job for the day is to bake and frost 100 cupcakes, as the anniversary cake shape will be created from an assemblage of these on a tier-shaped base. Our original plan was to frost half the cupcakes in chocolate and half in cream cheese. But that idea changes when Gayle goes to buy the premade toppings.

"I was so surprised to find this color alongside the basic types," she says, showing me a can with turquoise cream frosting inside. "I knew you'd agree with using it instead of the white. What a coincidence! It matches the color of our plates, napkins, and other decorations exactly!" And it does, to a T.

We get to work on our culinary project – mixing up

batter, baking, cooling and frosting the mini cakes. Our motions become coordinated and smooth. About halfway to our goal, we are discussing the ice cream cups that will also be served.

"They are all in the extra freezer on the deck," Gayle says. "I ran out of room in here."

Her words trigger an image in my mind of stacked up little Dixie cups – and a feel of vague unease. "I'm going to go take a look at them," I say impulsively.

I do and am dismayed by what I find. All the ice cream is melting! For some reason, the contents of each cup is soft, and sticky liquid is starting to drip down its sides. We have just enough time to grab all the containers, clean them up, and move them safely to another freezer, avoiding a sweet catastrophe.

Literal or Symbolic

Significant coincidence varies by verbal accuracy. Meanings of messages may be based on their actual wording, or in contrast, on something the words represent. Synchronicity may be literal or symbolic. Sometimes the Universe speaks to us in traditional, exact ways. We easily understand its messages and the meanings they convey. But sometimes things are more metaphoric, and meanings derived solely from figures of speech.

Though we'll delve into the challenge of distinguishing these differences later on, it's good to note now that words do not always mean what they at first seem. It appears the cosmos uses whatever language best expresses its wisdom, whether literal or symbolic.

Synchronicity about Synchronicity

An exploration of the two main types of synchronicity, messages and materializations, and their varying characteristics should include a look at a third and most unique combination type. Synchronicities about synchronicity seem to be both materializations and messages. When we become aware of coincidence and start watching for it, the meaningful experiences increase. Our focus on the events serves as an asking for more. And when we become fascinated by the subject itself, the coincidences often concern the same.

Sometimes these are simple instances of hearing or reading something about the subject shortly after we have been thinking of it. Materialization examples in response to our thoughts. The Universe arranges things to give us what we seem to want, based on these thoughts, coincidentally. What is amazing is how quickly we may come across written or spoken accounts of synchronicity once we are concentrating on it, well beyond selective perception.

December, 2010, Salem: I have begun playing with the idea of writing a book on synchronicity. While considering this, the idea is almost continually in my thoughts, in the back part of my mind anyway. I check out a few novels to read for enjoyment and a little distraction. Immediately, on the first page of the first book I start, a character experiences a meaningful coincidence.

Another book I am reading is a true adventure story. The author tells the tale of a serious accident that resulted in an impressive coincidence. She came away knowing that some kind of higher force was in charge of her life.

Since making the definite decision to write this book, synchronicities I experience have changed. Like these mentioned titles, almost every book I read, even seemingly unrelated ones, have some reference to the topic. What is different now is that there is often additional discussion or speculation about coincidence on top of the descriptive anecdote.

A few months later I am reading a mystery. A character in the book experiences several unusual things, and is curious about their meaning. Were they really coincidences at all, she wonders? Or messages from a higher source? I read her words and feel puzzled too, about my own experiences. These coincidences about coincidence are becoming increasingly complex.

It's as if they are both manifestations of my focus as well as answers to whatever personal questions I currently am asking about the subject, plus ongoing reassurances of its validity. And why not? Certainly the Universe has the ability to multi-task through its own messages! Hopefully I'll pick up on these multiple layers of meaning when they occur.

About the same time, I come across a most fascinating book. *Psychic Roots: Serendipity & Intuition in Genealogy* it is titled. The author, Henry Z. Jones Jr., was early bitten by the genealogy bug it seems, when as a child he discovered an old trunk full of family mementoes. While still in high school he wrote his first book on the family tree, and for him the rest – as they say – was history!

Later, as a professional genealogist, "Hank" became intrigued with a group of families called the Palatines, who emigrated to colonial New York from Germany. After diligently tracking and documenting these ancestors, he published several comprehensive books of their lineage. And amidst all his research, between the pages of his projects, he noticed something curious.

Unforeseen forces often seem to play a part in the research process. A big part. Personal intuitions or hunches frequently lead to information that would not have been found in any other way. Coincidental events, of which researchers have no control, guide them to fortunate and unexpected finds.

These discoveries may be anything helpful – a misplaced or improbably stored record, a previously unknown ancestor, an eerily alluring time period or place. Whatever the find, synchronicity and serendipity seem to play roles. Hank wondered if there is a psychic aspect to research? If so, do our ancestors ask for understanding and a chance to tell their tales?

He decided to find out, personally experimenting by listening to his inner voice and following his hunches. And to his great pleasure, paying attention to his sixth sense often brought surprising rewards. So he went further, writing to other genealogists, asking about their exper-iences.

In particular, he wanted to hear about any fortunate coincidences or intuitions they may have come across in their research. And the response was amazing. The result was the publication of *Psychic Roots*, in which more than a hundred respected historians related their experiences and made a good argument that having thoughts and feelings about our ancestors results in more success climbing the family tree.

I've read the introduction to the book, and am eager to hear its stories. A few serendipities of my own, that happened some years ago while researching come to mind. Then the thought – I wonder if I will experience a synchronicity while reading this book on the same? A coincidence within the coincidental accounts that is personally meaningful? Not likely, I conclude.

In the first few pages the author tells of his earliest discoveries. Family history portrayed through old photos, letters, and other treasures in the antique trunk. How he expanded his inquiries, finding more treasures and clues in other family members' mementoes. His diligence then paid off. "I eventually discovered a tattered pedigree chart made by my grandmother in 1882," he explains, "that took my father's family back years before the revolution, and one line (the Fullers) eventually to the Mayflower."

What? The FULLERS? To the Mayflower? But these are *Eric's* Fullers, too. Hank's ancestors and my husband's are one and the same? A surge of disbelief races through me. Then they must be distant cousins or something. A feeling of amazement takes over now with the realization that

THIS is the coincidence within the coincidence of which I thought a moment ago!

What's most perplexing about this occurrence is the timing. How could the whole thing be arranged by whatever so fast? I mean, I just considered the possibility of experiencing a pertinent synchronicity while reading about the subject a minute ago. There's the matter of the book's existence. The contents of *Psychic Roots* were already written and published long before I thought of my question, including the all important bit about the Fullers' line that constituted my coincidence.

Maybe higher forces knew ahead of time that I was going to be considering this idea? Or the question was percolating in my unconscious and it responded to that? By arranging the example - drawing me to the book. No way to every know the answer to that, for sure. I do know, however, that I feel great about the confirmation of the process and am mightily impressed with the conjuring.

5

Thinking, Speaking & the Magic of Words

As a kid, I had a favorite word – "cream." How this gem was chosen is a mystery to me, but I was bedazzled by its apparent brilliance. Quite simply, it was the very best word ever, that's all!

Back then, the sight for me of the word itself could bring up delicious visions of creamy, whipped fluff. And dreams of its velvety texture to taste and touch. I even loved the tone of the word when spoken, which sounded as rich and felt as smooth as what it meant.

Those quirky imaginings led to an early fascination with words. Special terms and phrases whose meanings felt good. And to the opposite as well, words I disliked for their effect – how bad they made me feel.

All of us have them. As adults, we continue this game of learning words then adding to their basic meanings. Providing terms, sometimes unconsciously, with our own special slants. Being around others, we can see those variations. Connotations created and understood sometimes only by ourselves.

Take these individual interpretations of words among a couple of women I know. One gal has a favorite term for truly troublesome stuff. Whether outer or inner pressures, when her "plate is full" she's stretched to the limit. When life goes completely crazy and nothing seems right, viewing the whole thing in this way makes it more understandable and easier to get through.

Another woman hates the slang term, "whatever," when spoken in response to comments. She feels the phrase is rude, implying something personal about the original speaker. And to her that feels bad. Whether or not others mean it that way, or as a simple comment of disinterest in the topic, doesn't matter. Her interpretation is personally true and firmly in place.

What are Words?

Things we rely upon and use continually can seem like a given – something sure and always there. Like words. But what are words really, and how do they arise? And is remembering these facts important at all? I think it is.

Words are signs of language, of this we are sure. Sounds evolve into words or units of meaning used in writing and speaking. Words, in a few of the same, are symbols of ideas and things that make up language.

As titles of meaning, words stand for something. Or for several things. They may have single or multiple associations with concepts and objects, and with each other as well. Because of their ability to evoke strong feelings, it is no surprise that some traditions have attached a magical power to words themselves.

September 2013, Salem: One of my favorite reference

books, a thesaurus, is falling apart. It's not a common title and was published back in the 1960s, but I love it. Its simple layout and abundant synonym listings are helpful. Comparing its word meanings to those of current guides, I somehow manage to choose what works best in my writing. I really want another copy of the exact same old book.

Some of these are probably for sale online. But I am impatient and would really like another copy now. Like today. So when I flash on the name of a little used book store across the river, I decide to head over. Once inside, I find their tiny reference section that includes an assortment of a dozen or so dictionaries and other titles. On the bottom shelf I spot the familiar silver-papered spine of my favorite thesaurus. Eureka! This one, though, coincidentally, is in fine shape.

Why are Words so Important?

As symbols of language, words are essential. They allow us to think, understand and share. Without words as tools, we'd be unable to reflect and reason or to communicate as well as we do. Because words stand for things, words allow us to store meanings. This permits comprehension – understanding ideas, objects etc. – and thinking, or knowing what things mean. And they allow us to express ourselves, communicating our notions and thoughts with others. As thought deals with meanings, word symbols are necessary for it all.

Words, in essence, provide us with personal choice. We can reflect on things deliberately when making decisions.

They offer us true independence in life by allowing us to act from a place of careful consideration instead of spur of the moment impulse or appetite. Words are necessary for language, and language for thinking, and that pretty much says it all. We need words to help us think, understand, and communicate.

September 2005, Portland OR: I am at one of my favorite places, the behemoth "City of Books" store, *Powells*, downtown. Like usual, I am contentedly browsing the metaphysical section. The huge selection of new – and more fascinating to me, *used* – books is eclectic, always with something of interest.

As I scan the rows of titles, checking out the most enticing, a couple of browsers are talking nearby. One says something about the *New Renaissance Bookstore* to the other.

The business sounds slightly familiar, and I assume it is local, but I am not sure if I have been there or not. If so, it must have been some time ago. Anyway, the name of the place is interesting, and I like its connotations, so make a mental note to look into it later. And then get back to my browsing.

A couple of minutes go by then a title catches my attention. I pull it from the shelf in front of me for an inside look. Once in my hands, I see that something has been tucked between the pages, which fall open to that place. And there is the name again, *New Renaissance Bookstore*, printed on a bookmark. A little thrill runs through me at this deliberate feeling nudge, and I note again mentally to check out the place.

Oddly enough, I never do. Maybe because when looking for books in Portland I usually go to *Powells* and end up with an armful of books. The store is enormous – multi-leveled with numerous giant, color-coded rooms – and holds enough fascinating stuff to keep me amused for hours at a time. By the end of each visit, about half a day or so, I am satisfied AND tired.

So the thought of investigating another location, bookstore or not, is pretty unappealing. But maybe that wasn't it at all. Maybe I just forgot about the coincidence and my ideas about it, until seeing it again in my journal.

January 2014, Salem: I am reading through my records, looking for coincidences that tie in with this chapter. I run across this one, happening over eight years ago and am surprised. Whatever was this about I wonder? A simple overheard remark plus a randomly found paper? Was I being prompted toward info of some kind at the twice-mentioned store? The whole thing certainly felt that way, like a gentle yet purposeful nudge towards, well, something.

Or maybe it had more to do with the words of the store themselves, *New Renaissance*. I take a look at other journal entries for the same period and see that yes, this was a time of change. My Internet bookselling business, in operation for nearly a decade, had been closed. And the future was wide open.

I was exploring work options and interests and trying to decide what I wanted to do, truly a point of renaissance or beginning again. So the words may have been a message of encouragement to go ahead and try something new.

In the middle of these thoughts I decide to look up the word in some dictionaries, curious to see if the meanings listed might spark added insight. So I choose a handy paperback edition and randomly open it to – "Renaissance." The word I am looking for is not only on the exact pages I happen to open, but the very first word listed as well! Plus it is boldly printed as a guide word for the page in the top margin.

Renaissance's definitions, I read, include *revival, re-birth, especially of learning and creative achievements*. That word "learning" sparks a knowing that this is about my study of coincidence. And encouragement to pursue it in ways that are new. I sense too that this series of message may not be finished yet.

6

Different Perceptions, Different Preferences of Words

We all experience life differently. Most of us are aware that people perceive the world in individual ways. Some take in information mostly by sight, some by sound, and some by touch. And each prefers it that way.

Though theories abound about thinking, our own observations are the most accurate judges on the subject. We see that everyone understands things uniquely. Through our preferred perception we process what we've learned – mull it over – think about it. And share our reality with others.

It follows then that individuals depend on varying aids to make sense of their worlds. For sight perceptors these are written words and images; for sound perceptors, spoken words; and for touch perceptors, activities, which also leads to different affinities, our natural likes and skills. This makes perfect sense when we remember the three main ways of understanding – sight, sound and touch.

So what does this have to do with coincidence? Is it helpful to us at all? Will being aware of our thinking style assist us in understanding our own synchronicities?

Absolutely yes! From my experience, knowing how we personally obtain and understand knowledge is not only helpful, but necessary to fully gain the benefits of our own meaningful coincidences. Here's why.

If we know our perceptual preference – the sense through which the majority of our information is received – we are more likely to recognize synchronicity. For the nature of these events varies, sometimes a lot. Coincidences may be big and dramatic. Or subtle and small.

To make them noticeable, the Universe communicates through our personal reality channel. After all, it's our primary way of knowing – paying attention to the world. When we are aware of this, we can actively work with the phenomena by deliberately questioning and then watching for answers within our mode.

If we know our sensory preference, we are more likely to understand the gist of coincidental meanings as well. This is the way we think, comprehend, make sense of life. We are also more likely to remember the events themselves, when perceived through our favored sense-ways.

This can be especially helpful if the meaning of a synchronicity is not immediately understood. That feeling of significance is remembered, and our minds mull it over, unconsciously anyway, with a good chance of a Eureka! moment later on. But this can't happen if the whole thing is forgotten.

And most importantly, when we know our favored perception, we are more likely to grasp the entire message of a coincidence, all its levels of meaning. Within our perceptual element, we reflect and deliberate best. If a synchronicity has multiple layers of meaning, we are most apt to understand and experience its fullness here. And tap into the self-discovery and other opportunities it provides.

Understanding Styles – The Bottom Line

So yes, different personalities appear to experience different types of coincidences, with varying types of – drum roll – WORDS. Sight perceptors, estimated to be around 65% of the population, with their emphasis on seeing the world, mostly experience syncs involving WRITTEN WORDS and images. Sound perceptors, approximately 30% of us, rely on speaking and hearing and have synchronicities of SPOKEN WORDS. And touch perceptors, estimated at 5%, are helped by movement, experience coincidences including WRITTEN or SPOKEN WORDS, while being active.

Of course, we use all three channels to perceive, think and share. But one is often dominant and our preferred way of operating. That smoothly spills over into our relationship with coincidence. When we know this sensory channel, we are steps ahead in knowing how messages will arrive. Bottom line: coincidental information from the Universe will often arrive via the type of WORDS used by our understanding style.

Discovering our Understanding Style

Many of us are already aware of our preferred way of "seeing" – how we take in experiences and think about them. What we notice the most in our surroundings and what we are attracted to. How we reflect, imagine and communicate. But if not, there are lots of clues to help us figure it out.

This in itself is valuable, for more self-awareness is good, as it often leads to self-development of some kind. And, more important for our purposes here, it helps us to become aware of the nature of our syncs. We will investigate perception types in later chapters, exploring the details and style of their synchronistic events. But first let's look at some clues to discover or reaffirm our own perceptual preferences, which will take us there.

As already touched upon, things we like and are attracted to are often easy for us. And fall within a style. Related activities and objects tend to be visual, auditory, or kinesthetic. As a sight perceptor, we often like pastimes involving written words or other images, and are good at them. A sound perceptor tends to enjoy things with spoken words and other sounds, and also find them easy. If a touch perceptor, we often are involved and good at activities with both types of words, along with some kind of activity.

Another way to look at this is through mood. Sometimes when doing something within our style we flow – entering our personal zone. Nothing else seems to matter because we are right there in the moment, engaged in an enjoyable activity that feels right and easy. Though this doesn't happen all the time, when it does, it's a clue that we are where we should be, upon our perceptual path.

Along with this is the opposite clue of difficulty. Perceiving and understanding outside our dominant sense-way is often awkward or difficult. Consider these examples.

Eric, sight-oriented, found songbook instructions worked best when he was learning to play guitar. He needed permanent written images of diagrams and words from which to study. Videos, combining demos of players together with spoken instruction were not as effective.

Another friend, who is sound-oriented, found exercising at home difficult, even with visual video instruction. She discovered classes combining jazz with routines much easier and that the mixture of music, conversation and exercise to be very enjoyable as well.

My mother-in-law, who was touch-oriented, loved to gamble. While at a casino, she particularly liked to try unfamiliar slots. If confused, she would turn to someone and ask, "Do you know how to play this machine?" Then, the combination of their instructions plus her hands-on experimentation would teach her what she needed to know.

Another angle of this clue of difficulty is annoyance. By noticing what circumstances or personality traits of others pushes our buttons, we can understand what reality seems most true and feels most important. When others don't place as much significance on things that are seen, or said, or done, as we do, it can be irritating. After all, from our way of thinking, these are the things that count the most!

Thinking Style Lingo

A fun way to discover or reaffirm our perceptual preference is to notice descriptive language we habitually use. Not surprisingly, each of us often uses key words and phrases related to our sense-way when we write and talk. Each way of thinking is expressed in terms that offer cues to its dominance; sight, sound, or touch.

For instance, visually-oriented people often use words that reflect their viewpoint, such as "look," "see," and "appear." They describe stuff – objects, activities, ideas, whatever – based on mental images. So their understanding of a concept may be "crystal clear" or "somewhat muddy." Then, with more explanation they might "get the picture" or "see what you mean."

Sound-oriented people experience things differently. Their sensory viewpoint is often reflected in words such as "hear," "listen," or "tell." They describe things based on mentally imaged sounds. So, in our example their description of understanding a concept may be "clear as a bell," or conversely they may "not hear what you are saying at all." In fact it may all be "just idle talk."

January 2014, Salem: I am looking at my notes about this topic of key words used by perceptual types. One phrase suggested by Eric for sound perceptors, "strikes a chord," catches my attention. I think to myself that it is uncommon and I doubt too many people would say it. A bit later I am reading my email. A note from Deidre, my auditory friend describes something that really "strikes a chord" with her. OK. All right. Got it!

Back to our discussion of key phrases and understanding types. The third category, touch-oriented people, often use terms related to feeling or moving. They describe things based on mental concepts of contact or action. Their favored sense-way is often reflected in words such as "feel," "hold" or "touch." In our hypothetical example of idea exchange, a touch perceptor might respond with, "I know how you feel." If uncertain, they may have trouble "getting in touch with what you're saying." And if the idea annoys them it might be described as a "pain in the neck."

Perceptor Style Quiz

Here is a short questionnaire to discover or reaffirm your dominant perceptual mode. Each question's answers suggest sight, sound, or touch perceptors respectively:

1. If attending a flea market, you are most aware of: the sights of people and merchandise; the sounds of conversation and the room; the activities going on around you.

2. If watching a play, you are most aware of: the actors' costumes; the actors' dialog; the actors' movements.

3. If remembering a family picnic, you first recall: the sights of the people and park; the sounds of talk and nature; the activities of those attending.

4. If remembering a visit to the coast, you first recall: the sights of the ocean and beach; the sounds of the waves and gulls; the feel of the weather and sand.

5. When learning to do something new, you prefer to have: written or graphic instructions; spoken instructions; a demonstration of it being done.

6. When studying a book, you prefer to: read silently to yourself; read the material aloud; do some kind of other activity while reading.

7. When making a decision, you prefer to: research written sources; ask others their opinions; actively try out different options.

8. When talking to others, you are more apt to agree with their comments by saying: I see what you mean; I hear what you are saying; I understand how you feel.

9. After conversing with others, you first remember: how they looked; what they said; what they were doing.

10. On a vacation tour, you would be most interested in: the sights pointed out by the guide; the stories told by the guide; the activities going on around you.

11. You prefer: descriptive or illustrated books; recorded books; action-filled books.

12. You remember best when you: see new information; hear new information; physically participate somehow with new information.

13. When watching a video, it annoys you most to temporarily lose: the clarity of the picture; the sound of the story; the movement of the film.

Let's play with these thinking style differences a little more. Using the example of a day at the beach, we can imagine how each of the three perceptor types could typically experience a synchronicity.

For instance, someone who prefers sight input might find an abandoned beach towel or graffiti-covered stone while sunbathing. The words or images on the objects feel meaningful and answer some current question or need.

Another person, preferring sound input, might hear the comments of strangers on the beach, that are pertinent to current concerns. The overheard remarks convey a message and feel oddly meaningful.

And someone who relies on movement or touch to take in info, who is busily beachcombing, might come across a message written in the sand. The stick-penned sentiments are somehow significant for the viewer as well as the author.

Of course, we are just playing here, imagining the kinds of scenarios that might happen to different people. But in reality they often do, with surprising regularity. Synchronicity, it appears, however and wherever, is perceptually personal. As personalities vary, answers accommodate. Coincidentally, as we prefer to perceive, so we often receive.

7

Sight Perceptors & the Written Word

Are you a sight perceptor? I know I am. According to statistics, around two out of three of us are. With this sensory orientation, written words and images are important to us and how we take in information. Reading and seeing are our favorite ways to understand things and learn, to experience life, and our preferred way to share ideas about reality, the way we see it, to others.

For our purposes here, exploring some varieties among sight perceptors can be helpful. If we know some common traits among their personalities, it will be easier to know the kinds of synchronicities they are likely to experience. How and when the coincidental answers will occur. And where, in what surroundings.

After observing, researching and exploring synchronicity for many years, I have discovered a couple characteristic types common to visually-oriented people – investigators and artists. Though these two personality types are hypothetical, based on my personal studies, they often can be easily recognized through an individual's questioning style and values, where someone looks for answers, and what they prize most holds the key.

Investigators value truth and wisdom about the world and its inhabitants. They want to understand what's real about life, themselves, and others. Reading and seeing are important to them because they look to the written word and other images to answer their questions.

Artists value beauty, the loveliness and grace of things. They want to enjoy what's pleasing to the eye in their surroundings and other things. Reading and seeing are important to them and they often look to written words and images for answers.

People of either category may display the traits of their type in subtle or obvious ways. For instance, investigators might express their basic nature of wanting to know by being generally curious about most everything they experience in life. Others might focus their investigative nature on a hobby or career.

Likewise, artistic visual perceptors may express their desire for beauty in a general way, preferring attractive environments and choosing surroundings that look good to them. Others may focus their artistic nature through spare-time hobbies or professional work.

Investigators

With their inquiring natures and preferences for written words, it's natural that many investigators love reading and BOOKS. What better place to find exactly what they want. These literary types go by many colorful names.

January, 2013, Salem: Eric and I are driving to town, discussing this, the literary investigator type of person. We mention a few terms commonly used to describe these people – booklover, bibliophile, bookworm. A freight train begins crossing our road. As it chugs along, we notice that most of the cars are covered with enigmatic graffiti. Then one car rolls by with an understandable message. "BOOK-MAN!" it shouts out. Oops. Forgot to mention that one!

So what's the big deal with books anyway? To bibliophiles and avid readers, they are priceless. And essential. To sum up a shared sentiment, such people cannot live happily without a surrounding of books. Literature does hold an unlimited number of possibilities for us between its bound pages – possible ways to live, to understand ourselves and others are portrayed, and a tantalizing collection of old and mysterious clues about the cosmos along with modern concepts about it.

Books are a record of history, wisdom and ideas, of all we have discovered and thought. All we have tried, all we have gained, all we have ignored and lost.

We literary types turn to books for many different reasons. Sometimes it is for entertainment, the enjoyment of an adventure or humorous story. Sometimes for knowledge about a myriad of varying things. And sometimes for magic, the discovery of hidden truths and exciting thrills. Books, with their words and ideas are indeed priceless and powerful.

December 2011, Salem: The following three events are

more examples of the many coincidences occurring throughout the writing of this book. The cluster happened during the planning stage as I am envisioning the book's focus. At this time, I definitely know its subject will be synchronicity but not the principle in general.

There have already been a few non-specific titles written on that to be of some help to readers. I am more interested in specifics – how coincidence occurs to individuals – the differences happening between people. In particular, how the coincidental language of words varies from person to person.

So, with that unspoken question in mind – are the WORDS of synchronicity truly important for our understanding of them – I go about my normal business which includes much reading. At the library, I check out an interesting looking older book, *The Haunted Bookshop,* by Christopher Morley.

Though I recognize the titles of a few of the author's other books, I am not really familiar with him or his work, beyond the fact that he wrote in the early 1900s. I don't take time to read the synopses of this book either; I just like the look of its quaint cover art and assume it is an old-fashioned ghost story of some kind.

But it's not. When reading, I discover that the title, *The Haunted Bookshop,* does not pertain to the supernatural but to "the ghosts of all great literature." The novel, published in 1919, centers on the adventures of a Brooklyn bookseller. Throughout the book, there are references to literature's benefits of knowledge and wisdom and the "ghosts" of the past that haunt places where books are stored. To Roger Mifflin, the bookshop owner, the total meanings of books' words are significant as well as palpably present.

This alternate message surprises me at first, and then it doesn't. I randomly chose a book to read in which characters repeatedly discuss the importance of words conveying ideas from within the pages of books. And the tremendous benefits to readers of books which somehow seem to "find" them. Roger Mifflin explains, "There is no one so grateful as the man to whom you have given just the book his soul needed and he never knew it."

While the book I am envisioning may never do all that, it will offer some new ideas on the meaningfulness of words we coincidentally receive. And to me, right now, Morley's novel reminds me through its characters' musings that people find what they truly want or need from the book they "happen" to read. How great is that!

This sync was so fun to experience, that a day or so later I am thinking of it while writing out seasonal cards. My address book features quotes on friendship as a decorative element. I just get started when I notice that the first quote featured on my needed address page. It's author – Christopher Morley.

I've never really paid attention to the quotes in the book – it's a newish one, and I mostly look up snail mail addresses during the holidays – and I might have seen Morley's name there with his quote and filed it mentally somewhere. What is odd is that I happen to need an address for the first card written that takes me to the Morley quote page. And right when I'm thing of *The Haunted Bookshop* theme and its coincidental relevance. Very peculiar indeed.

A day or two later, this pertinent theme of the importance of words appears again. Deidre emails me an account of a fascinating literary mystery. It seems that during 2011, a group of ten mysterious paper sculptures had been discovered in Edinburgh. Each intricate piece was created from old books and had been left in various Scottish libraries and museums. An accompanying gift card expressed sentiments in different ways, honoring ideas, words, and books.

This last link in the coincidental chain of three, affirming the importance of words, tickles me. Each incident not only conveyed the idea of the very real significance of words. It also used them in a written form to synchronistically answer my question.

How are synchronicities likely to be conveyed to literary people? Through the written words of literature. With their love of books and the printed page, bibliophiles spend a great deal of time with both. Whether they avidly read for pleasure, or as part of their work – book collecting, selling, writing, reviewing, editing, etc. – literary types relish the experiences an author's words provide and the limitless menu of ideas they convey.

Where are these events likely to happen? Anywhere a literate person interacts with books. Libraries and book-stores are naturally popular, serving a comforting second home to many. But private homes and offices are common, too – anywhere really, spent browsing, reading, or working with books and other printed matter.

And when do they happen? Is there a time more likely for their occurrence? Apparently, whenever the Universe feels is the perfect time to answer. Through the printed words of books that bibliophiles love so much. The best response through the best book to convey the best coincidental message.

Researchers are a second common investigative type. Like literates, they value information and knowledge, and favor reading and viewing. Consequently, they look to the written word and other images for answers. These people may express their nature in different ways – through a general inquisitiveness, a passionate hobby, or professional work. It seems there is an infinite number of things for them to question, look into, and understand.

Think of researchers as anyone who personally centers on figuring the whole truth out about most everything, from everyday personal experiences to other people and life itself. Their interests may be scholarly or scientific – centering on recorded or viewable data. Or more wisdom-seeking – striving to understand the mysteries of life. In either case, researchers often look for answers through what they read or observe. And the Universe obliges.

Where do meaningful coincidences occur for researchers? That depends on the characteristics of their interests. Those who focus their investigative nature through a pastime or job are likely to experience them where they are working. And those whose inquisitive temperament is expressed in a general overall way may be their recipient most anywhere, depending on the research-ing incident or activity involved. But all researchers, re-gardless of their differences, will receive their personal messages at the best possible time for them.

Back when I first started considering writing a book on synchronicity, the references to it popped up everywhere. In particular, since I am an avid reader, in books of all kinds. As I've already mentioned, it didn't seem to matter what kind of book I was reading – novels, memoirs, whatever – the subject of meaningful coincidence came up.

Since it took more than a year for me to definitely decide to research and write about the phenomena, some of these events were of a general nature, an affirmation of the rightness of my decision. And others, occurring a bit after, concerned the specifics about the topic I was interested in.

December, 2011, Salem: I am doing a great deal of research about coincidence, but am still somewhat undecided about my focus. We have gone to Jason's for Christmas. His friend Joe is there too, and gives me a gift. When opening the package I am amazed to find an older looking divination set with an accompanying booklet entitled, *Chien Tung, Chinese Fortune Sticks: The Oldest Known Method of Fortune Telling in the World."*

It consists of a cylinder container filled with numbered bamboo sticks, plus a collection of corresponding quatrain answers. A brief history of the system is given in the booklet. It explains that the Chinese have long practiced this very personal method not as a game, but a naturally based spiritual art, that the method is simple but significant, based on a wisely understood correlation between the events humanity and nature. And carried out symbolically through the fortune sticks. The set is undated with no manufacturer marking of any kind.

What is uncanny is that Joe knew nothing about my proposed synchronicity book or the fact that lately I had been considering experimenting with divination tools a bit, said to trigger coincidental answers. Truly surprising!

A few days later, I decide to try out the set. After reading the suggested instructions I center my mind then ask, "Is receiving this tool somehow related to my research and writing?" Then I shake up the sticks within their container and draw the first one that jumps out. In the answers booklet, I find the interpretation for the stick drawn speaks of shortly being inspired, originating a project, and succeeding as an author of the plan. Fascinating.

December 2012, Salem: I am driving on a road adjacent to the freeway, on my way to do some shopping. The writing of this book is on my mind, particularly a question about it: What is the best way to keep the entire project fresh and fun like it is right now? I decide to ask the Universe and then watch for possible answers.

I do, then immediately see a billboard for an amusement park, *Enchanted Forest.* It reads, "7 *Miles Ahead.*

Fun! This startles the heck out of me. How fast the perfect answer to my query coincidentally appeared! It feels meaningful, and I intuitively know pertains to me actually entering the "enchanted forest" to write my book, that place where mystery and magic reign. Live in flow by following the surprising synchronicities of my own path, not just analyze and describe them in writing.

In addition, the phrase *7 Miles Ahead* speaks to me. Seven has always been my number, as my birth day, numerological life path, and a myriad of other things. To me, the words on a couple of levels refer to both myself and my personal plans for writing the book. And finally, the word "FUN!" is the perfect finishing touch to this pertinent message. Identical wording as used in my question, it really stands out.

Artists

In addition to investigators, artists are a second commonly seen characteristic type of visual perceptor. With their appreciation for beauty of all kinds, and its reliance on sight, it is not surprising that they might also prefer written words. And look to them as well as other images for the answers to their questions.

Artistic types of people may express their nature in a variety of ways. From general admiration of surrounding beauty – good design, pleasing lines and balance in nature and manmade things – to personally creating. From hand-crafting enjoyed as a hobby, to professional artwork pursued as a career. Along with innumerable other art-related possibilities like collecting, appraising, selling etc. In any case, meaningful messages are coincidentally received through visual words and images.

Where do artistic types experience synchronicity? Most any place, if their appreciation is expansive. For there are no limits to forms and objects and designs of all kinds pleasing to the eye. For these people, who value beauty in an overall widespread way, syncs may occur through written words or other images, anywhere they happen to be.

Practicing artists and others with art-related particular passions may do the same but also may experience insights while involved in their work. Through its visual images or written words of some sort. In any event, every artist will experience meaningful coincidence at precisely the best time to convey its private message.

December 2012, Salem: The author of a book I am reading is discussing money, specifically how a friend of hers always seems to find lost cash, coins and bills in any denomination, when she asks the Universe for them. Wow! I think. That would be fun and handy. This gal must be seriously in sync.

The next day I mention the story to Eric and say that of all coins, what I seldom find dropped on the ground or other places, are nickels. A little later he is raking leaves in the yard. Through the window I see him pause to pick something up. He brings it inside and hands it to me. "Here is your nickel," he says.

Eric's synchronicities usually involve images. As an artistic type of sight perceptor, his meaningful coincidences often include pictures – mental or physical – as well as words. This talk of coins and images brings to mind another incident that occurred on an outing.

We have gone to Silver Falls to hike. The park, a gorgeous recreational area nearby, encompasses several thousand wooded acres accented by musical Silver Creek. The stream meanders noisily along, sustaining lush foliage on its banks. Trails crisscross the water, winding through mossy tree limbs and stones. Feathery ferns flourish everywhere, quenched by the sparkling mist of the falls. And that is the best part – the falls.

Within a few miles of walking distance are nine or ten wonderfully different waterfalls. Amazingly tall and silvery falls with their tinkling streams, to wide and soaking falls with thunderous roars. And there's more in between. We are walking along the creek, enjoying the day and the sights when I spot something curious.

There's a shapely tree stump, prettily textured in earthy greens and browns beside the trail. Someone has decorated it with a penny. A shiny, new copper coin standing on edge, wedged into the center of the wood, looking discordant yet strangely symbolic of, well, something.

I immediately think of the phrase "In God we Trust," that appears on U.S. coins, plus the background beauty of Mother Nature, and wonder if someone was trying to express the same. Probably not; I do think a bit differently than most. I call Eric to take a look and he does, then he whips his camera out to take a picture of our interesting little discovery.

Later, on the way back down the trail, Eric decides to take more shots of the stump, viewing things from his artistic way of seeing. But he is too late. Someone has driven the entire penny flush with the wood. Was it a kid, I wonder, maddened by a coin that wouldn't come loose, to pick up a rock and hammer it completely down? Or some other artistic type bothered by the image? A few explanatory words carved into the wood underneath would have been thoughtful...

Spring, 2012, Gold Lake, OR: Deidre's husband, Adam, has gone fishing. The trip of a few days has taken him into the Cascade Mountains that dissect the state. He really enjoys the beauty and peacefulness of the area, a perfect place for fishing and quiet thoughts. As he sits in his boat on the water, he thinks about the move to New Mexico that he and Deidre are considering. So much is involved – there are important considerations and complications – is it the right decision?

Suddenly there is a commotion overhead. A large V-formation of Canadian geese is noisily flying south. This is unusual as flocks normally migrate in the other direction around this time of year. Adam knows this is his sign, that moving to the southwest is the right thing for them to do. And he feels good about that.

Sight perceptors. They share a preference for what they

read and see with their own two eyes. Yet express every difference imaginable in their personalities. Though researching and artistic temperaments often are visual, so are an unlimited number of other types of people.

But in spite of some differences, we may benefit most by noticing similarities. How we perceive, how we think, how we understand. By sharing in some of these stories we may recognize ourselves. And our likelihood of receiving coincidental answers through written words and images.

8

Sound Perceptors & the Spoken Word

Are you a sound perceptor? It is estimated that about a third of us are. With this favored perception, oral words and other sounds are important to us, and how we receive information. Speaking and hearing are our preferred ways to understand. To experience the world – life itself. And our favorite methods to communicate – share our views of it with others.

As in our discussion of sight perceptors, exploring some varieties of sound perceptors can be helpful. Similarly, if we are aware of some common traits among their personalities, it will be simpler to anticipate the kinds of synchronicities they are likely to have. How and when coincidental messages will occur, and in what locations.

I have observed a couple characteristic types that seem common to sound oriented people – social people persons and musicians. While these two personality types are essentially hypothetical, they often can be recognized in our direct experience through their manner of questioning and their values. Where they look for answers and what they hold most important.

People persons appear to value sharing information and or helping others. They want to exchange their thoughts, feelings, and ideas through conversation and to or to contribute through activities beneficial to others. Speaking and conversation are important to them, and they often look to the spoken word to answer questions.

Musicians value the beauty of sound – the rhythm and tone of instrument and voice. They want to enjoy what is pleasing to the ear – melodious and harmonious mixtures of notes. Because hearing is important to them, they also often look to the spoken word or other sounds for answers.

People of either category may exhibit the traits of their type in evident or not so evident ways. For example, people persons may express their basic nature by being social or helpful to most everyone in their lives. Others might channel their verbal or caring temperament through hobbies or work.

Likewise, musical sound perceptors may express their desire for beautiful sound in a general way, surrounding themselves with melody and music-related activities. Others may focus their nature through spare-time hobbies or professional careers.

People Persons

With their helpful and social nature, it is natural that many people persons love talking and listening to others. What better way to exchange supportive info and personal opinions! As their favored means of communication, the spoken word is where they often look for answers. These people may express their nature in different ways – through an overall sociability and helpfulness, a favorite hobby, or professional work.

I think of people persons as those who personally center on sharing their ideas or active caring with others. They may work in fields of education or persuasion, such as teachers, salespersons, public relations etc. Or those of empathy, such as therapists, theologians etc. Or in a more general way, predominantly using personal conversation in all aspects of their lives.

Where do synchronicities tend to occur for people persons? That depends on the characteristics of their interests. If their social or caring nature is focused through recreational activities or work, syncs are likely to happen there. If expressed in a more widespread way, they can happen anywhere, depending on the activities involved. But all people persons, regardless of small differences will receive coincidental information at the most ideal moment for them.

February 2010, Portland OR: Jason has recently ended a close friendship due to differences in important personal values. He and a new friend attend an event featuring beautiful ethnic music. Jason mentions to his companion that at least he won't run into Ms. Ex-friend here, as she dislikes this kind of music.

A moment or two later, said Ms. Ex-friend walks in, coincidentally and amazingly (Portland is home to more than 2,500,000 people!), with a companion of her own. Jason is astounded. Then he overhears her sharing opinions of the same sort that he previously found troublesome. You two will always have irreconcilable differences no matter when and where you happen to be, the Universe seems to say!

October, 2011, Salem: I have changed the names of some contributors in this book. Every incident related in it is true, of course, but some identifying characteristics have been changed for privacy.

I decide on "Deidre," for some reason, for one good friend. This is odd in itself, as I have never know anyone named Deidre and seldom even come across the name in reading. Nonetheless, I do, and over coffee tell her this. She smiles and says, "When I was a kid, a little girl named Deidre lived across the street. I loved her name and always used to pretend that it was mine!"

She tells me of another coincidence involving spoken words that happened recently. "When I was visiting my daughter Sara in New Mexico, we went shopping. And found an interesting shoe shop to browse. I spotted a really cute pair of red shoes at the same moment she did. Then I looked at the price and told her they cost too much.

"Sara talked me into trying them on. They fit perfectly - and were, coincidentally, the ONLY pair left in the store. The clerk did some checking and found out that they just happened to be marked down as well! So I bought the shoes, since they were seemingly there just for me."

Musicians

In addition to people persons, musicians are a second

commonly seen characteristic type of auditory perceptor. With their appreciation of melodious sound and its reliance on this perception, it is not surprising that they might also prefer spoken words. And look to them for the answers to their questions.

Musical types of people may express their nature in a variety of ways, from general admiration of harmonious and melodious notes of voice or instrument to personal music making, from singing or playing pursued as a hobby to professional career, along with numerous other music-related possibilities – teaching, collecting, selling etc. In any case, meaningful messages are often coincidentally received through spoken words and sounds.

Where do meaningful coincidences occur for musicians? That depends on the characteristics of their interests. Those who focus their musical nature through a passionate hobby or professional work are apt to experience them where they work. And those whose musical temperament is expressed more generally may receive them nearly anywhere they are enjoying or involved with music. But all musician type people will receive they synchronistic messages at the most personally choice time.

February 2011, Salem: I email Deidre, telling her about a talented pianist I recently heard playing a song of boogie woogie swing. My friend is a pianist herself, as well as an enthusiastic teacher of the instrument. Deidre responds that she happened to teach her student the rhythm for boogie woogie just today – and that the song they practiced was the same one I mentioned.

9

Touch Perceptors
& Both Types of Words

Are you a touch perceptor? A small minority of about 5% of us are estimated to be touch perceptors. With this favored perception, either written or spoken words may be how we receive information. Moving and touching are our preferred ways to comprehend things and to learn. As long as we are doing one or both of these, we are better able to understand written or oral messages of all kinds.

A few characteristic types that may be common to touch oriented people include those who like to work with their hands – mechanics, builders, sculptors etc., and those who thrive on movement: athletes, sportsmen, dancers etc. This includes anyone who appreciates in a general way or focuses a hobby or work through movement or touch, or anyone who enjoys action, and does best with a hands-on learning approach.

And when do synchronicities tend to occur for touch perceptors? Whenever they are involved in activities using their favored perception. I haven't personally known too many of these personality types and have only been close with one of which I am aware – my mother-in-law.

Winona grew up on a rural farm in southern Colorado.

Though money was scarce, the two girls of the family, Winona and her sister, enjoyed horseback riding and dancing when they had the time. There were chores to be done at home and school to attend, for a while anyway, but they were active most of the time. And that was how Winona seemed to best understand the world.

A few years later, as a young mother with a husband in the service, she was naturally busy. When he died shortly thereafter, Winona and her sister hitched a house trailer to their Chevy sedan and headed west. This was in 1945, pre-Interstate, and the two-lane blacktop roads were sometimes rough or even dangerous. The little family of four, the two women and two children, nonetheless successfully crossed the Midwest to the Pacific, ending up in San Diego, partially due, it seems, to some fortunate coincidences along the way.

Though Eric, as a small boy at the time, doesn't remember much more than playing with his toy trucks alongside the road, his mom always did. She told of overheated engines, flat tires, and other difficult scenes – and strangers who knew what to do just happening to stop. To help the young sisters or give advice, exactly when they needed it.

Later, as a working mother, Winona kept up her active preferences. She worked as a drive-in carhop, a cook, and a city bus driver. She danced and rode horses and took the kids on picnics and trips. And she relied on trial and error to learn what she needed. Though she never remarried or won the lottery (she lived to be 100), she always believed in good luck. I wish I would have asked her more about those coincidences that convinced her of it.

Personal Types of Coincidence

After exploring the variations in our perceptual prefer-ences – sight, sound, and touch – we see how they often go along with either written word or spoken word or combination word syncs. The way we perceive often correlates to our special type of coincidence.

Our personalities, too, serve as clues, particularly what we value and enjoy. But personality types are guesses by logic, really. So our best bet is to go by our intuition. What synchronistic type seems like the best fit for us? What feels like our natural style of these three ways of receiving higher guidance probably is.

That being said, it is obvious pretty quickly that the Universe doesn't always communicate with us in the exact same way. For whatever reason, the circumstances vary. But if we know our usual messenger – written words, spoken words, or combinations of both – we are steps ahead to recognizing and understanding these cosmic answers. Consider the following couple incidents, which occurred in non-typical ways.

January 2014, Corrales NM: Deidre relates this coincidence communicated visually, instead of through her favored sense pathway of sound. "I was walking to my mailbox, which is quite a distance from the house, and thinking about you, in particular of a recent section you had written for the book. Right then I saw a landscaping truck parked on the road that I had never seen in the neighborhood before. It's business name – 'The Ace of Spades.'"

September 2011, Salem: Eric and I are running errands and shopping in town. We somehow forget to go to the bank as planned. Later at home, we open our mail to find an unexpected check that needs to be deposited at the bank anyway. This helpful incident does not contain any visual elements that usually play a role in my husband's and my synchronicities.

10

Lifepath, Passions, & the Joy of Flow

"In the flow," "go with the flow," "in the groove," "in the zone." These are common expressions that many of us use to describe a most pleasant state. It's apparent that when we go with the flow we feel good and experience positive results. But what is flow exactly, and how does it operate? What can it offer us? And how does it relate to coincidence?

Though there are different ideas about what makes up flow, its true meaning always lies with us. Our everyday experiences will show its personal reality. Being in flow is usually a fun and focused place. When there, we are immersed in what we are doing and enjoying it. Things are easy and smooth. During periods of flow all facets of our lives may be affected.

We may recall memorable stretches of time – hours, days, weeks, or longer – when we glided through our life's inner and outer events as fluidly as water in a placid stream. While experiencing a deep sense of harmony and joy, all the while focused on our current endeavors, completely in the present.

During times like this, when we are in sync, events happen as they should. Things seem to just fall into place.

Everything clicks. Obstacles disappear, and abundant coincidental clues appear to serve as our guides. Our desires and needs are easily fulfilled and answered. During these periods we see that life in indeed full of meaning and magic. And works in surprising ways.

What creates this all encompassing flow? Our personal connection to the cosmos, specifically to the energy field, the prana that permeates us and everything in our world. When we are in tune with this life force through our intuition, we are plugged in to the power and knowledge of the Universe. And everything comes together. Synchronicities abound when we focus and follow our intuitions in flow.

Lifepath & Passions

Many spiritual and philosophical traditions throughout history have taught that we are all born with our own lifepaths. According to these teachings, each of us has a pre-chosen mission or purpose. When we are on track, it seems, knowingly or unknowingly following this blueprint, our lives work and we feel good. When we're not they don't. It's as if there are markers along the way to keep us on our true paths to accomplish our goals for this lifetime.

Our special destinies can be recognized through our talents and passions. What do we find easy and love to do? Where do our talents and interests lie? These special offerings of ours have often been present since childhood and often are the subject of some of our favorite memories. When we look back it is easier to see our personal gift –

what has always been unique to us and a little different than the skills of others? Where do we always find enjoyment and deep involvement? There lies our path.

This important track for each of us involves the sharing of our particular uniqueness with others. What we love to do most is our gift to the world. When we do this – help others by pursuing our strongest passions with an eye toward their well-being – everyone gains and we are happy.

The Universe helps us find our direction through synchronicities. Coincidental guidance occurs to point the way. These messages from the cosmos aid us at every step of the way from discovering our purpose and path to staying on course once we do. Sometimes these prompts are unexpected and surprising.

November 1992, Monterey CA: I awake in the night and am astonished at what I have been doing while asleep – composing the melody and lyrics of a song! Part of a catchy little tune and simple rhyme still runs through my head. A voice mentally asks, "Don't you know how good you'd be at this?" (No I don't!) Some of the lyrics linger:

What WORD is you; When best you do; I'm the motivator, I'm the motivate me!

I lie there thinking about it, and the way I am when at my best – no roles, no doubts, just me. And my feeling of excitement about the unlimited possibilities in this surprising world of ours.

And about the voice in this experience, which does not feel strange at all, I remember similar narrators commenting on current questions or concerns with helpful suggestions. Just the year before, in fact, in a dream that stayed with me, a voice calmly stated an idea I had long debated about my personal path. "You can help the most people through your writing," it said. I hope that opinion is true!

Sometimes coincidences occur to let us know that we are on the right track. Synchronistic messages confirm for us we are heading in the right direction to fulfill our purpose. Or they may clarify a point of confusion about a track we thought was ours but now are doubting. The following guidance occurred to answer a question about my literary path.

September 2005, Salem: I have been freelancing on the Internet, writing for a couple of websites. Though my articles, mostly on the subject of home decorating, have been pretty popular, they are not what I want to write. Inwardly, I've been questioning how I can earn my income researching and writing about metaphysical topics, exactly as I choose?

With this thought in mind, while puttering around the kitchen, I open a new package of herbal tea and select a bag to brew a cup. I see that each teabag has an attached tag with a phrase written on it. Curious, I look at the one I pulled that advises, "Use gentle words and firm reasons." Hard indeed to disagree with that wise solution!

November 2012, Salem: While in the beginning stages of

researching this book, the literary guidance continues. As a divinatory experiment, I decide to consult the tarot with a question about my synchronicity work. To begin, I relax, focus on the query, then ask, "What's the most important thing for me to do with my research and writing?" Then I shuffle the cards a few times from the set I own, *The Zerner-Farber Tarot Deck*, by Amy Zerner and Monte Farber, and draw one that catches my eye. Turning it over, I see that it is the Princess of Hearts.

The deck's suggested meaning speaks of the need for me to concentrate on the communication of personal intuitions, loving feelings, and dreams. To creatively express passionate ideas. The message of the card I coincidentally drew is uncannily meaningful, saying that writing about my intuitive take on synchronicity is not just highly enjoyable but the very thing I need to do.

When we are on course doing what we should be doing, the Universe helps us stay there by offering tips and solutions. Jason's friend Joe tells me the following story:

"My mom Lou was visiting me from out of state. At the time, she was an elementary school teacher of third graders. My mom is really nice, a kind and generous person, and she really cared about her work and kids. She was always looking for ways to make the best learning experiences for them.

"Anyway, to make things easier, she came up with an idea to help her 24 students carry chosen art supplies back to their desks – small handled trays. She shopped around and found some, a group of bargain-priced used platters of a perfect size and shape for little hands. She bought the entire lot, a dozen in all, and had been wishing ever since that there had been more.

"While she was visiting, I suggested we go look around a second-hand store. We did, and Mom checked out the housewares section. Amazingly she found a stack of the sought after trays, same size, same style, even the same palm tree pattern. And when she counted them there were just the right number that she needed, another dozen!"

Interestingly, I learn of this coincidence at a personally pertinent time. While working on this chapter, I am looking for illustrative examples of path-related syncs. Jason has Joe share the story with me after hearing it first himself. I immediately sense how the sharing of it answers my current needs as well as the actual event did for Lou. Double punch.

Sometimes synchronicities communicate about the essence of our lifepaths instead of its concrete details. Coincidences serve as messages about the FEEL that following our path provides. These meaningful episodes may happen when we are initially searching for our direction, on our path, or at a crossroads. They can happen too when we've somehow gotten completely off course. It's as if the Universe explains that the easiest way to stay on course is through joy. What feels best, it seems to say, is YOUR special way.

June 2013, Salem: I have just gone through a particularly stressful event. Or what would have been, previously, anyway. I am going over the whole thing in my mind, to see why this time was different, while browsing at the library. A novel's title catches my attention, so I pull it off the shelf to take a closer look. The pages fall open to disclose a handwritten note, a forgotten bookmark.

The encouraging message was written by a stranger to her niece. Live with excitement, she says. Be bold – try adventurous fresh things, even if you may not succeed. Begin this year in a new way, knowing each day holds new possibilities for passion and creativity. Live with feeling – begin anew. I tuck the note back inside between the pages and close the book. Standing there in the tranquil quiet of the library, I realize that the letter was meant for me, too, right now, with a personally meaningful message.

The mystery writer says to live with passion, to do new things in your life. When you begin a new page, surprises can occur. And that's just what happened this time when I approached the stressful experience in a new and different way – unexpected and calm results. Inspiring, and personally true words indeed, coincidentally.

When it gets down to it, synchronicities involving our passions and purposes are some of the most important answers we receive. Coincidental words or circumstances relating to our path and its adventures can be highly meaningful. Sometimes they send tingles up our spines with their disarming sense of otherworldliness – even if we can't quite believe they happened at all.

March 2014, Walnut Creek, CA: Suzanne, a cousin of Eric's,

has died, and her sister Trudy relates this coincidence to us. "I was getting some of Suzanne's possessions ready to sell. There were tons of things to go through, share with family, donate etc. Things were going okay and the house was clearing, with the exception of a large library of books. Though an advertisement had been posted about it, so far no one had been willing to come and take a look. And that was holding things up.

She continues, "Then the realtor called with a weird story. Apparently the night before she had an odd dream. In it, Suzanne appeared, and told her not to worry about all the books still in the house, that the dilemma was being taken care of and a solution was in the works.

"A short while later a woman phoned and said she that she was interested in the books. She asked to come take a look at them. 'Sure,' I said. She did and liked what she saw very much."

What Suzanne had was an assortment of books including a bunch of Russian titles. It turned out that the woman herself was Russian, and had been wanting some books to help teach her children about the country and its language. "In just an instant both of our problems were solved," Trudy said, "and the books found a new home!"

So what does this have to do with lifepaths and their people's passions? Russia was evidently important to Suzanne's. During her lifetime, she visited the country several times and enjoyed learning about its culture and was learning to read and speak Russian as well. Did her strong interests in the location somehow enable her (from the other side) to be involved in the exchange?

Or was she instead a dream symbol used by the cosmos to deliver its reassurance? Either way, we will probably never know for sure. But what is evident here is that everyone concerned received what they wanted. Through the coincidental arrangement of events concerning the passions of people. People existing in different dimensions, no less.

As in other aspects of our lives, coincidences continually arise to guide us in these things we most care about. We are in sync with the Universe and not resisting its flow. Let's take a close look now how coincidental written words may deliver their myriad of meaningful answers to our wants and needs.

11

Written Word Synchronicities

It seems that words have some big advantages over other images as the messengers of coincidental answers. To begin with, we know so many of them. As our common signs of language, the normal way most of us think, comprehend, and communicate, we have to. It is estimated that average English speaking adults may recognize over 35,000 words, and some many more. Though most of us don't use all those words in our vocabulary, we still have a pretty good idea what they mean. And that's what counts.

On top of all the primary meanings are our connotations for some of them. Personal meanings based on our past experiences, or beliefs we have formed color or add more meanings to the words we know. This provides a gigantic set of building blocks with which the Universe can construct the perfect messages to us full of pertinent advice.

Of course, images of all kinds can be used to communicate as well. Symbolize things and express their multiple meanings. Along with words they play an essential role in both our mental and physical worlds. Nonetheless, when it comes to synchronicity, words are often the symbols of choice. Comprising or making up many meaningful answers.

Characteristics of written words used synchronistically are what we would logically expect. Coincidental clues arrive through our own writings or those of others. Words we have previously written expressing most anything, or words written by other people, deliver the Universe's answers.

These meaningful messages vary dimensionally through space, time, and form. They naturally vary in where they happen, when, and in what arrangement. Without getting too technical here, let's take a look at these common variants of written word syncs.

Public or Private

Sources of written words used by the world are virtually unlimited. It appears that any recorded information can be favorably used. These syncs can be roughly divided into those using public or private writings to convey their meaningful messages. It is utterly fascinating to imagine all the forms of public wording which might be employed to provide an answer.

Advertising, for example, is a huge source, with possibilities ranging from large types of ads down to small. Think about billboards, and business signs, and handmade posters. Vehicle ads and model names on cars, and planes. Or the brand names and manufacturers listed on most anything that we buy, of any size, from a giant screen TV, to something as small as a tiny pink eraser.

And then there's the wording on paper items, meant to be seen and understood by their readers. Books, often first to mind of course, along with magazines and cards. Newspapers, certificates, brochures – even junk mail. And other lightly worded things we might not think of as well, like coupons and paper money. Plus electronic pages – all the reams of information on the Internet through websites, ads, and blogs. When it comes down to it, anything with a message for the public is game.

December 2011, Salem: We have been involved in a minor car accident. At the time, we were taking my mom to the hospital to visit my dad, who had been injured. Luckily, no one was hurt in either vehicle, but our car has been declared totaled by the insurance company. Coincidentally, we find out, the party in the other car was also on their way to the hospital.

We are feeling pressured to find a new car. Our insurance does not provide a temporary loaner, and we currently are borrowing a relative's car to shop. Most of the time, our recent downsizing from two vehicles to one has proved advantageous. But right now we are a little stressed by the complications. Was paring down really the best thing to do?

I have checked out a book by Robert Moss entitled, *The Three Only Things: Tapping the Power of Dreams, Coincidence, and Imagination.* In between car shopping I start to read it. Immediately upon beginning the book, I am hit with some right-on coincidental advice that addresses what is going on with us now. Moss states in the Introduction that if we can keep from feeling sorry for ourselves and ranting when "bad" stuff happens, we will usually discover some kind of unique opportunities or other positive results within the events.

He continues to relate a sync recently experienced in which his jeep gave out at an extremely inconvenient time, and he had to quickly buy a new rig. Then, once on the plane (where he was initially headed),he was seated by a woman who related a similar simultaneous tale. This whole emphasis on damaged vehicles, coupled with fast and furious car shopping mirrors our current predicament closely, of course. Surely the best approach is staying cool while noting the humorous aspects of it all.

Adding to this synchronistic cluster, an acquaintance, upon hearing the news, asks me if our insurance company is going to provide us with a rental car. "No," I say then continue my reading of the book (from our borrowed vehicle while Eric roams the car lots).

I learn that the author's airline flight conversationalist described herself as someone who advised adjustors regarding rental cars being supplied for people who have totaled their cars. Ditto. We quickly do end up with positive results from the episode. Like Moss, driving away from the confusion in an intact, well-running newer car.

Sources of personal words are equally vast. Though not as visible in our everyday lives as those of public inform-ation, they exist nonetheless in private locations reserved for the eyes of individuals. As non-public or even secret writings, belonging to oneself or meant for particular people, private words abound.

One of the first sources of private words that comes to mind is letter writing. Through traditional notes or through emails we express and we share. Like with coincidental public writing, privately written words used will be those of another person – their beliefs, experiences etc., or those of ourselves. Sometimes even our own words are used for answers. Whatever the source of the private words, however, other people or ourselves, we will end up with a new idea, insight, or info. Meaningful information that we didn't have before.

Journals are another possible source of written words. The Universe may use entries from our own diaries or those of others to send us messages. Likewise lists of all kinds, copied maxims, quotes, etc. Even a word or two scribbled on a scrap of found paper.

The common denominator here is that all written words are game. Words written privately for the non-public. Graffiti is another source available for these symbols. Though flamboyantly displayed, it is usually made up of private words meant for a particular few. As is marginalia, written by readers in book page margins. Offering opinions only to a similar group (who are reading the same book that is).

Present or Past

Another way to understand coincidence is through the dimension of time. Synchronicities may involve writings from current, past or antique words. With this immense pool of historical material, the best words may be collected and polished by the universe to display the perfect gem of a message.

At first thought, it seems that current words would be predominantly used for coincidental answers. But on second thought, maybe not. Higher intelligence chooses its vocabulary from within our habits and interests, so messages come through these forms.

If we are literary-minded – readers, writers, scholars, etc. – our personal syncs are likely to come at times through literature of most any age. But if our interests lie elsewhere, current wording through non-literary forms is likely. Each of us, overall, probably will experience coincidences using words from both present and past sources, even if one period predominates.

May 2014, Salem: Eric and I are driving in town when I spot a curious truck. It pulls rounded silver storage compartments and is totally unmarked. "Does that truck carry milk?" I ask. Eric thinks that it might but doesn't think it looks quite right for that. Suddenly, at the intersection another truck buzzes across. "The Milky Way" it brags on the side-bed with images of the creamy white stuff. My answer is clearly, No, THIS is what a milk truck looks like!"

Synchronicities through words written in the past include those from many literary sources. In our modern age of super rapid change, much is outdated as soon as it is printed. Past writings may convey ideas, beliefs, and circumstances different then our current ones. Sometimes vastly different.

June 2007, Salem: I have bought a big bunch of old letters. The collection of 35 pieces from the late 19th century was offered for sale at an online auction. And I really wanted to own it. Looking at its contents now, as it has just arrived, I am curious and eager to read the letters; and certainly not disappointed by what I see.

Most of them, obviously written by different people, are in pretty good shape. Many of the cream-colored pieces of paper are still crisp and clean. The inks that flowed upon them are quite readable, having faded from original colors to sepia. Old-fashioned handwriting varies from elaborate styles with curlicues and delicate flourishes to decisive lettering, both plain and bold. Reflecting the various personalities of the penmen perhaps.

I'm not sure exactly what is the allure of these letters. I do love old paper. And they surely appeal to my curiosity about things unknown. More though than dipping into someone's life is the thrill of looking through a clear window into the past. Stepping back in time, in a way. And viewing real life events from there. Then being left with some kind of nostalgic wonder over the other-timeliness of that place.

So I peruse the letters leisurely, reading maybe half of the group. And share a few of them with friends over conversation and tea. And each time I read I am entertained or humored, enlightened or saddened, or sometimes simply amazed. Because these letters writers back in the 1880s are, well, human. This sounds ridiculous, I know, but when all we have to go by are facts, a time and its people fall flat.

But when the news of the day is shared by those who experienced it in their own words, all that changes.

So over a few weeks time I read some of the letters. And I think about them. I know there is *something* that needs to be done with them, or rather that I need to do with them, of that I am sure. But I never quite figure it out so eventually file the whole bunch safely away. And pretty much forget about it.

Fast forward seven years to May 2014. We are in the middle of a major household de-cluttering project. I am going through all the paperwork – evaluating, filing, discarding etc., when I come upon the letters. My mental antennae perks up. Oh yeah, the *letters*. I still need to read them all, for some reason. A faint feeling of importance follows this thought, so I follow it by pulling the papers out of their storage for a look and later in the day get down to it.

"Dear, dear Josie," one began; "My Dear Uncle," another; "Dearest Daughter," another yet. When it came to salutations of letters in the late 1880s, not much has changed from what we might say if we wrote a traditional letter today.

Then something a little different, a combination report of receipt and appreciation of the personal relationship. "Received your letter day before yesterday, bet I was glad to hear." Or "Right happy was I to receive strong assurance of friendship, sympathy, and love." And "Received your welcome letter and so pleased to hear from an old friend, true and tried!"

Sometimes there was a thank you for a gift or favor previously given. "Your letter of the 16th with $4 inserted arrived next day eve – it came timely for I had not a cent and had to borrow." Or, "Received the sweetest little package a few days since from the sweetest girl I know!" There may have been mention of a gift being sent by the writer as well, such as "You will find enclosed a white silk handkerchief."

Next in these messages was often news of the writer's health and that of her or his community. "I take my pen in hand to drop a few lines to let you know we are all well." Another, "There has been a great deal of sickness in this town." Or "I thought I only had a severe cold, but bless my soul I whooped!" And, referring to the children, "The change of air, food, and water this time of year might be bad for them."

There often were health warnings and concerns regarding the recipient, "You need to be careful" and "Hoping to find you enjoying the great blessing." Sometimes they related requests, "Let Mother and sisters have what money you and Charlie can spare to get them comfortable wraps for the cold weather."

Most of the letters contained news of all kinds concerning the life and locality of its writer: "The weather here is mild. Had a splendid pineapple for dinner, with oranges every day." Or another, concerning day trips, "We can go either by steam or electric car."

The news sometimes was of general concerns, "Vassar has a great many new students this year," or shyly personal,

"We have a little baby. Her name is Elmira." And of other apparently pertinent information, "I am sorry you did not take your old pants."

Sometimes there were complaints but sometimes humor as well. Concerning a toddler: "This is not very good ink as Edna got it and a bottle of Aunt Flo's medicine and emptied them together!" Or, "So the lasses 'O caught you with taffy hands sticking together!"

Oftentimes complimentary, "I became a foot taller immediately upon receiving your letter." Ending with a heartfelt request, "As I cannot sit with you all around our own hearth...." "Write often – I depend on you for all the news." And finally the closures, "Your affectionate Pa," "Ever your loving daughter," "My love to yourself and sister" etc.

I come away from the reading of the letters with mixed feelings. They are fascinating and revealing. I feel I understand these people, who laughed and loved and lived their lives nearly a century and a half ago, a little better. I also am struck by the sense of family closeness the letters obviously convey. The thread of health and tender concern for one another's well-being that winds its way through the messages.

There obviously were lines of connection firmly in place for these people even when physically far apart. It gets me wondering – are family ties truly stronger than other relationships? I have never thought so. I always have believed that it is the commitment and energy invested by those involved that determines the bond. But these letters have got me reconsidering.

In the middle of my musings, Eric received a phone call. It is Sonia Sue, a distant relative of his, though a virtual stranger. Eric and Sonia have not seen each other since childhood, more than fifty years ago! Turns out Sonia Sue is framing a portrait of another relative as a gift for her own mother and wonders if Eric can fill in a couple blanks. Does he happen to know when this ancestor was born and died?

He helps her the best he can then tried to personalize the conversation. "How great it is," he says, "to connect with a relative you have lost touch with!" But Sonia Sue is not interested in pursuing this train and quickly brings the conversation back to her project then terminates the call.

Eric shrugs the whole thing off, but the incident feels very strange to me. Why would someone phone a recently relocated relative and NOT want to get to know them – at least a little? It makes no sense. But then suddenly it does. Just because they are FAMILY doesn't mean they are interested in closeness or even expending the effort to create it. Ties between people depend on mutual desires of the heart, not bloodlines. Thank you, Universe, for the reminder! The message for me through the old letters seems complete. But is it?

Sources of written words used synchronistically can vary tremendously by period. Coincidental messages are conveyed through all kinds of old and new writing. Current sources are easy to imagine because we live in the modern world and are familiar with them. Past or historic ones, other than literature, are harder to imagine. If we know that we are particularly in tune with written words, it pays to be attentive to any sources of them we happen upon, whatever their age.

When we are earnestly looking for answers, the world will respond through our favorite form of communication and written words. And these words may appear on old objects as well as new. So during these times it behooves us to be alert to tangible things with added words as well as to books, paper and the like. Including things from the past or long ago. Objects we see, anywhere – antiques shops, museums, even graveyards might provide the answers we are seeking through their coincidental old words.

Literal or Symbolic

Another way synchronicities differ dimensionally is in form. Their messages may be literal, symbolic or figurative. Answers may be exact in meaning, made up of words representing something else, or composed of any number of figures of speech. The determining factor as to which form a sync takes may be clarity. Sometimes the literal meaning of coincidental words says it all. Other times the answers to our needs and wants are more complex and a non-literal message communicates this best.

Literal responses often result from quick questions or simple requests. If the information we need is uninvolved, these answers are common. The messages are often short if our question is easy, but not always. Sometimes lengthy amounts of info are literally conveyed. The key is that the Universe can answer our focus with a one-faceted message through traditional meaning words.

May 2014, Corrales NM: Deidre writes me about this fun incident. "Adam and I were discussing a man he knew who was terrible about monopolizing conversations. It seemed you could not get a word in edgewise with this guy. Adam commented that my daughter (trained in classical languages), probably knew a good term for a guy like that.

"Later in the day he was reading a novel and one of the characters was described as having 'logorrhea' or a tormenting wordiness. Voila! Then a couple of days later he was reading another book and came across the same word a second time. Adam was sure he had never seen it in print before, though here it was again. Point taken. Question, coincidentally, quickly answered."

Symbolic syncs, in contrast, are numerous and often used to convey more complicated answers. The cosmos seems to select symbolic words when there are multiple levels of meaning to impart. By using them as signs that stand for several coinciding things, we are provided with wisdom on multiple personal levels as well, such as the physical, the mental and the spiritual.

Sometimes we spontaneously understand all levels of words used symbolically, and sometimes we don't. The message of a meaningful coincidence may unfold for us over time. Or occasionally, though feeling significant, remain undecipherable to us until some future Eureka! moment.

Spring 2000, Salem: Eric and I are walking through an unknown neighborhood. I am upset about how I reacted in a recent situation. Specifically, I ask, "Did I act like Ms. Such and Such? Remember, she is the one who some years ago left the unforgettable trail of hurt feeling among my circle of friends?"

He starts to reassure me. "No," he says, "nothing like that." I begin to ask for his insight into what really happened, when I notice the sign for the upcoming street. "Ms. Such and Such Street," it reads, titled with the same unusual woman's name as the subject of our conversation.

Uh oh! I feel a jolt as the parroting of this name registers. The sign speaks clearly as a symbol of all the unwanted personality traits. As it appeared in the middle of our talk, it seems to confirm that I acted similarly. Or does it? More to come later on this one.

The next incident portrays a different type of coincidence entirely, in which the symbolic words appear mentally to lead to an answer.

May 2014, Salem: I own a vintage 1950s Mexican silver bracelet. I'm not sure where I got it, and the busy design is kind of strange – not really my style at all. It is not worth a lot of money, but does have some collector value, and I'd like to sell it. Just not through the Internet for various reasons.

A local consignment shop is a possibility, as they work for a worthwhile cause and do a good trade. Their percentage take is pretty high though, so I'd have to price the piece accordingly to clear much of anything at all. I know its online value, as there are several bracelets like it for sale on a website. What I wonder what it might bring in Salem.

For some reason, I start thinking of a pawn shop I often pass while driving. In particular, their sign out front advertising, "We Buy Gold." The letters of that sign keep flashing through my mind every time I think about the bracelet at all. Though it certainly isn't gold, and not too valuable, it does have vintage appeal. Maybe they can give me some kind of idea of its value, or their own interest in buying it by taking a look?

I decide to visit the shop. Once inside, I see that despite their gold buying sign they really have very little jewelry. There are a couple display cases filled with a variety of rings, but very little else. Then I spot another small case displaying half a dozen or so vintage pins, and, on closer inspection, one other piece. A Mexican silver bracelet identical to mine! I am flabbergasted and naturally pleased. What a local business evaluates the piece for is now plainly evident, and helps me to price my bracelet more accurately for local consignment. What better answer could I received!

Figurative

Figurative communication is a third form synchronicity can take. Messages through written words may be full of figures of speech. These irregular forms of expression are used to create special effects through the language **they** use. Literary devices play with words and phrases to produce particular results. They use specific words or the positioning of them to aid understanding or stress a point. Sometimes they use wordplay to create a feeling or mood.

For instance, a coincidental message might use hyperbole, or words that exaggerate, to evoke a strong feeling, or metaphor to create images with descriptive words. It might convey humor through a pun, using words with several possible meanings, or understanding through similes paralleling two unrelated things. Any type of literary technique or a combination of devices may be used to catch our attention and communicate a perfectly pertinent answer to us. The Universe plays with words as tools to get its message across.

My synchronicity concerning our search for the old movie, *A New Leaf,* was an example of this. When I saw the billboard proclaiming "Relief of Leaf!" the rhyme and exaggerated silliness of the phrase instantly made me laugh at myself for the big deal I was making over not being able to find the film. All with two simple words and a little punctuation. Sometimes though, the play on words is considerably more complex.

June 2014, Salem: It's the old letters again. One of my favorites from the bunch, a correspondence from a father to his son, is still in the back of my mind. The letter was both colorful and sweet in news and sentiment. Its writer was smart and very lonely. Away from home over Christmas, staying in a boardinghouse, he entertained his family with imagination and expressed concern for them all.

Antiquated phrases and references were used in the letter, and I find them fascinating. Wanting to know more, I look up some of the terms and events. Then I go a step farther, researching online the gentleman's name and location, coming up with a probable match on a genealogy site. My thoughts turn to Trudy, Eric's cousin, deeply involved in family history. I write her an email describing the letter and my curiosity about it. Maybe she would have an idea about some of its statements if she took a look? "Sure," she says, "sounds fun, send it along."

Meanwhile, Trudy is going through papers of her own. Applying for membership to a genealogical society, she is putting together required documents. In the middle of this my letter arrives. Trudy takes time to study it, and emails me her opinions. Then gets back to her own project – until something startling occurs. She phones us immediately.

"My great grandfather, and yours too, Eric," she says, "fought in the Civil War. He was captured in the South and imprisoned by the Confederate army at Andersonville. Though only there a few months, his health suffered, and he was left permanently disabled.

"For which he tried and failed, for many years, to obtain a pension. I have here a letter written by a friend who served along with him. It's a notarized statement of our great grandfather's worthiness for receiving his pension. And dated almost twenty years after their release. But here's what's freaking me out – it was written by the same guy who wrote that old letter you just sent me!"

Unbelievable! I am speechless a minute, trying to get a handle on how this could be. "You're kidding!" Eric says.

"Oh, wait a minute," Trudy goes on, "It might not be the same person after all. The first names are the same and the middle initials, too. I think the last names may be one letter different, though. You know old handwriting. So what do you think?"

I think the whole deal is incredibly weird - and feels significant, somehow. And I'd love to see this second letter.

So Trudy sends me a copy of it, and I compare the two papers, concentrating on writing styles and signatures. I agree that they were written by two different men with nearly identical names who, coincidentally, showed up in my experience during thoughts of family ties.

Apparently the incident of a distant relative appearing in our sphere after 50 years wasn't a clear enough message. A guy with a similar name to my old letter's author had to pop up and point out the other side of the coin: family ties don't necessarily create a bond – caring and kindness and commitment do. And what's between good friends are sometimes the strongest bonds of all.

12

Spoken Word Synchronicities

The words we use are powerful because we think, speak and write with them. Feelings we link to words based on personal experiences, or those we hear about, give them the ability to affect our lives. Deliberately chosen words are a powerful tool we can use to clarify our understanding, wants and needs. Maybe that is why life uses them as coincidental messengers.

Characteristics of spoken words, like written words, are what one would logically expect. Coincidental clues arrive through our own spoken words or those of others. Our thoughts, our statements, and those of others deliver the Universe's answers. Through mentally or orally uttered words. Like written word incidents, these meaningful messages vary dimensionally. Differing in when, where, and what arrangement they happen.

Public or Private

Sources of spoken words used by higher intelligence are practically limitless. It's apparent that any discussed info can be favorably used. These syncs can also be roughly divided into those using public or private conversation to convey their messages.

It is intriguing to consider the variety of public wording

which might be used to convey a response. Once again, advertising is a huge source, this time what's spoken aloud. Think about radio, TV, and theatre ads, as well as movies watched at home, plus Internet advertising of various kinds conveyed via audio.

Then there are the individuals selling something they publically proclaim: street vendors, telephone, and door-to-door. Plus those selling more subtly through speeches, seminars, etc. – you get the drift. The common denominator of all this advertising is the oral words they provide which may perfectly mean something to us. And without the sale of a solitary thing.

And then there are the words said aloud and in forms meant to teach or entertain. Think of radio, TV and movies again, particularly newscasts and shows. Or classes and lectures held any place at all. Then one of the biggest mood-makers of all – music – wherever it is played – its lyrics or spoken title able to coincidentally convey more meaning than expected.

November 2012, Salem: At home, I've been working some hours on my research and writing, particularly the question of synchronicity's validity. I decide to take a break and watch some TV. I flip through the channels randomly, then stop at a scene. It's a conversation going on, and I catch the word "signs." Naturally, I tune in as one character wonders whether circles appearing in his crops are there by chance or are signs of something watching us? His words echo my focus so well that I know they are a message for me too.

Though the movie turns out to be about extraterrestrials doesn't matter. A few words from it spoken right then answers my thoughts.

Sources of personal words are vast as well, through everyday talk. Conversations we have with others can carry messages for us within the words of our speaking partner. When we talk with acquaintances, friends, family or even strangers, there is always the chance our conversations may communicate far more than we anticipate. Coincidental comments by others may offer just the idea or guidance that we need. Deidre tells me of this helpful example.

October 2012, Salem: "After Mom died, I was disposing of some of her possessions. There was a pretty decorative plate commemorating the 100th anniversary of the church Mom had attended while living in Herrington, Washington. I got the urge to call Billie, a long-time friend of my mom's who still lived in the town and asked if she knew of anyone who might be interested in the plate.

"She quickly answered, 'Deidre, you are not going to believe this, but the anniversary plate hanging on the wall of the social room at the church was broken – and we haven't been able to find another one!'" Object lost, object found – coincidentally.

Sometimes those we talk with will be aware that they are providing information we want. But not always. Sometimes what they say will be a clear message for us without their awareness of it at all.

December 2011, Seattle WA: A friend tells me this story, as was related to her by Maggie, another friend. She begins, "Maggie received a phone call from Renee, a casual acquaintance, inviting her to dinner. She accepted, and the time was set. That evening, Maggie arrived at the appointed restaurant. Since she was early, she sat in her car while listening to the radio. A station was hosting a talk show. The subject under discussion was FAS, or Fetal Alcohol Syndrome, a condition in which unborn children may develop mental or physical defects after exposure to high alcohol levels."

She continues, "Later, when Maggie and Renee were having dinner, Renee shared the sad story of her adopted son who it seemed could not connect his personal actions with consequences. This was a huge problem she said, the source of ongoing behavior issues. 'How strange!' Maggie responded, 'that sounds like what I just heard about on the radio.'

"She went on to tell her friend all about the program. The two soon moved on to other topics and finished their dinner. But the message conveyed coincidentally had apparently hit its mark. At a later date Maggie was reading her college bulletin and found that Renee was now active in support groups for families of FAS children."

Spoken word syncs also can be delivered anonymously via the words of strangers. Someone communicates a message to us without knowing it. They may be talking to a friend, conversing with a business colleague etc., and we will overhear the precise words we currently need. During these times when we are attentive and alert, the Universe may use an innocent person who shows up to speak the timely information we are looking for.

The ancient Greeks practiced a type of divination called cledonism or cledonomancy, based on coincidental events, including overheard remarks. The words of other people were observed as well as the words of gods. In modern times we might remember the importance that eavesdropping once held, and be alert for our own cledons.

We can form our questions, then go out into the world to listen. When we pay attention we often hear meaningful words, spoken seemingly by chance, through others. My sister Gayle reminds me of a funny and bizarre instance of this when we were growing up.

July 1962, Grants Pass, OR: "I was a teenager then, and of course you were younger. It was early evening – dinner time actually – and the family was getting impatient waiting for you. Then the phone rang. I grabbed it and answered. "Let me talk to Mom," you demanded from the other end.

"But where are you?" I demanded right back. "You are really late and we are all waiting to eat. Mom and Dad are really getting bugged. Janet will be here in a few minutes to pick me up for the movies. So, when will you be home?"

"None of your business!" you snapped. "Now let me talk to Mom!"

I came right back at you, "No! Tell me where you are."

"I won't!" you exclaimed, "because I don't like you, and

you're a dummy!"

I remember a brief silence while I thought about this. *Something* was off. Though, as typical siblings, we sometimes disagreed, but we did like each other at heart. And virtually never resorted to name calling. "Who IS this?" I finally asked.

"Who do you THINK it is?" came the exasperated reply. "It's Judy, of course." Then after another pregnant pause. "You are Diane, right?"

I couldn't believe this. "Uh no," I managed to say. "You must have the wrong number."

So what actually happened here? And what was the point? I, the little sister, was late getting home and the family was irritated, that is a fact. Big sister Gayle had important teenage plans that I seemed to be hindering. So when some other little sister called – also coincidentally late for dinner – she let me have it. Or rather let HER have it. And when this other little sister responded nastily Gayle got the word that maybe her own sibling was not so bad after all. But what, I wonder, did "Judy" come away with?

Past or Present

Spoken word syncs may use material from current or past talk, flowing through the dimension of time. Though most of the speech we hear is probably that of our own or other people's conversations, oral words of the past are also available. What an immense pool of knowledge exists in old or historical recordings of speech! Golden nuggets may be sifted out and presented to us in some kind of synchronistic form. Words spoken in the past can come alive for us in the present through meaningful feelings of worth.

Because the Universe bases its vocabulary on our interests, spoken word coincidences will reflect this. If our concerns are mostly with the present, messages are likely to come from there. If we have a bent for history, however, things may be different. Coincidental answers may be conveyed through things said in the past.

Literal or Symbolic

As with written word synchronicities, those involving words that are spoken differ dimensionally in form. Their answers may be literal, symbolic, or figurative. Their messages may be precise in traditional meanings or composed of words standing for something different. Or made up of figures of speech. The determinant seems to be which form will most clearly communicate what the cosmos wants to say.

Sometimes the literal meanings of words we hear convey everything we need to know. Other times we understand them best symbolically. The responses to our focus may have several layers of meaning that work the best to convey a complete answer to a complex question or need. Figurative wording works in much the same way. Using some kind of unusual expression within the speech for special effect to catch our attention, emphasize a point, or perhaps suggest a new meaning.

The lengths of coincidental messages don't necessarily indicate their complexity. Sometimes a simple, literal response may take many spoken words to share, Similarly, an answer of just a few words may be perfect to convey something more involved with several levels of meaning.

February 2013, Salem: I have started a volunteer job. Having previously enjoyed giving some time to worthwhile groups, I am looking forward to the friendly camaraderie that goes along with it. But it doesn't happen. After a few sessions, I realize that the mood and activities of this group are not what I was expecting at all.

I resign and find another position that looks like a totally different deal. A couple key members are introduced to me, who coincidentally have the same first names as two key players of the first group. It isn't long before I discover that names of members aren't the only thing these two groups share – their inner dynamics are similar.

I get the message. Signs are saying that this is NOT my time to volunteer, at least with an outside group. Whatever they are, or are not, doesn't matter, things just don't feel right. It may be that family or friends will be needing my help soon instead.

13

Combination Word Synchronicities

Though overall our coincidences will arrive via written or spoken words depending on our affinity, there will be times when they won't. Messages will consist of a mixture of both. Or consist of other combinations involving words and images. It's as if the Universe uses our preferred perceptual path (type of words) for recognition, plus some additional symbols for clarity.

In these cases, a combination seems to be necessary to convey the whole essence. Significance may be complex; meanings multiple. Words are used alone or with other images in ways perfect for us to personally notice the coincidence and understand it. The following two incidents employed mixtures of written plus spoken words, the first related to me by my friend, the second involving me too.

December 2010, Salem OR: "I have really been working with my meditation and breathwork," Deidre emails me (She also practiced yoga, and enjoyed reading on these topics when helpful information came along.). "This morning I told Adam about what I had learned about the healing qualities of breathwork. He was skeptical. A little while later, when one of my favorite body/ mind/spirit type newsletter arrived by email, and there was one particularly pertinent piece, by chance, on the power of breathwork."

June 2014, Corrales NM: I receive an email from Deidre. She is busy creating an attractive native landscape for her new home in the high desert, presently focused on a par-ticular bed. "It's just sand and rocks right now," she says, "with icky black plastic underneath. "As if you have to do anything other than withhold water to discourage plants from growing here!"

I teasingly write back that I think she should keep the plastic look. Just uncover the entire sheeting and glue lots of cheap plastic flowers onto it. She replies that probably while I was writing up my suggestions to her, Adam was suggesting the same thing, to keep the plastic in the bed and stick fake flowers into it. She ignored us – twice.

The following sequence cluster of syncs played out initially over a few days, then its language was reused a couple years later for related messages. Communication was through written and spoken words, my own and others, plus images of colorful patterns.

January 2012, Salem OR: I am driving to the crafts store to look at jewelry-making supplies. Recently having bought a rhinestone pin, I would like to convert it into a charm. The pin is a vintage piece, formed from multi-colored stones. Its flamboyant design really sparkles and shines. I love the pin and it makes me feel good every time I look at it.

As I drive along a truck passes by, its colorful graphics

showing and describing "freshly picked fruit and veggies." The image and wording remind me somehow of the jewelry piece in my pocket, with its vibrant rainbow of colors. So similar to the variety of hues of garden fresh natural foods.

November 2012, Salem: At home one evening, I become aware that I am humming a children's song about colors, and listing the various hues to myself. I have no idea why. A couple days later, I am rereading my journal and come across the previous entry of how the spectrum of fresh produce reminds me of rainbows. Ah ha! I have been making smoothies the last few days. And enjoying the array of colors of their fruits and veggies before blending. Hence the happy rainbow tune.

A few days later still, while driving, I see several clear and bright bows in the sky. Their appearance is impressive and a little uncanny. The repetition of the rainbow theme through images and words feels significant somehow. I think back over the past week and remember a conversation I had over what's the best diet for good health. Is this pertinent to that? Intuitively I feel it is – all those "rainbows" standing for the colored fruits and vegetables important to well-being.

Fast forward to June 2014. I am in the middle of a caffeine spree, drinking lots and lots of coffee over the last month. And not feeling my best because of it. Ideally I drink just a little brew – some days even none at all, and do well with that. But I'm off kilter right now. So I start the tapering down process that will get me back to where I want to be, mojo-wise. And look forward to feeling my best again.

One afternoon while gift shopping, I come across an unexpected display. Amid decorative and art supplies is a group of kaleidoscopes. They aren't fancy – their tube sides are simply covered with astrological print paper – but they are eye-catching. And I can't help but pick one up to play. Then stand there for five minutes or so turning the tube's end-piece to see the patterns inside.

Oh, they are pretty! As these things always are. Ever changing mosaic mandalas of transparent jewels. And as I watch the glowing pieces change to one rainbow design after another, I decide to buy one as my gift and another for myself. Because I like what I see and am reminded of, something.

Later in the day, Eric returns from bicycling. He tells me of rings he saws in the sky encircling the sun. Rings made up in part of rainbow colors. We learn that these circles are formed by ice crystals serving as prisms that separate the light. I learn something else as well. That within his words the rainbows are a reminder to eat my veggies!

There's a postscript to this story. I had told Deidre about Eric's sun circles. The morning after I write up this account she emails me about an unusual sky formation she saw on an early walk that was rectangular shaped – and in rainbow colors.

And here's another meaningful coincidence portrayed symbolically through a simple phrase (ice cream) and the image of a surprising person eating it. It is August 2009, and Eric and I are vacationing in the southwestern states. We have stopped at Moab, UT, a vibrant little tourist town to see the sights, and get a bite of whatever. A busy simple foods café catches our eye. Inside, we look at their menu for something that sounds just right, but nothing does.

Then we notice at the other side of the building a huge sign promising beaucoup flavors of "ICE CREAM." But haven't we already been eating more than a little junk food? Suddenly I notice a young woman eating a cone. She looks amazingly familiar. But who could I know so far from home? No one it seems.

Then she turns her head and looks right at us and it clicks – the clerk from the natural food store in Salem! We all laugh in recognition and surprise. Our message, it seems, is to indulge a bit more in the sweet stuff as well as the healthy, when the timing is coincidentally right.

Combination word syncs, similar to written word or spoken word ones, can take a variety of forms. The language used may be public or private, literal or symbolic, current or past. Coincidental messages that answer our questions or needs are conveyed in whatever mixture of words and images works best for us.

When we are aware of our own special coincidence style, the kind of words usually used to communicate with us, less common combination experiences will be apparent, too. The first key to unlocking any synchronicity though, is to be aware of what we're asking.

14

Asking & Attracting Meaningful Coincidence

Synchronicities happen. When they do, we can be sure of a couple of things – first, that an asking has occurred through our focus on a need or desire, and secondly, that right then we are in flow, connected to the Universal life force.

As to the asking, it may be unconscious or conscious. We may be totally unaware, or in contrast, completely aware of our mental questioning, even deliberately trying to trigger the process. As to flow, it is our connection with this intelligent cosmic energy that allows us to coincidentally receive these answers.

When we are following the energy, we keep to a path that feels personally right. We decide on its route by what feels good and true to us. And when we do, things flow, click into place, work out, thanks to intuitive prompts and messages from the Universe.

Of course we aren't always in sync with the source. Instead of smooth terrain we may experience many uphill climbs in our travels. The trick seems to be to ASK for higher guidance. To deliberately attract then access its significant answers. If we can do that our lives will be filled with more happiness, meaning, and coincidental moments of flow.

There seem to be mental states that are essential to flow. When that's where we are at, deliberately or not, syncs naturally occur. We might cultivate these states in our day to day lives as we learn the workings of coincidence. Paramount is focus, of course, on our question or need *without* negative static. When we concentrate on our wants with no interference from anger, doubt, fear, or other opposing emotions, we keep the connection. And the answers come.

Alertness and patience are two attributes absolutely necessary for experiencing synchronicity. If we are not aware of our surroundings, we won't even notice its occurrence in the first place. Knowing our preferred way of perceiving is helpful, but paying attention to all that goes on around us the best. Coincidence is seldom predictable.

The ability to calmly wait for an answer to our needs is essential as well. When we think we have to push to make things happen, and are unable to endure any delays, we miss out. The Universe's answers to us through meaningful coincidence will show us the easiest, fastest, and most direct way of getting what we want, if we are patient enough to watch for them.

Openness and flexibility also seem to be necessary. The way the force chooses to answer us will often be a surprise. When we are open and accessible to how a message may come we are less likely to miss unusual means. And when we are adaptable to when and where it occurs as well, we are less likely to miss the unexpected.

Sometimes when we are not really conscious of our asking, these essential states are happening spontaneously. We are openly alert and flexibly patient to what is occurring around us. We are not blocking the flow of the life force with pushy attempts at control. And synchronicities occur naturally in this environment with pertinent messages for us.

December 2011, Salem: Patticake, one of our adopted feral kitties has been in some kind of scuffle, probably with another cat. He is upset and slightly injured, and won't come inside. I finally manage to coax him into the shed, where there are plenty of places to rest, and he spends some time there.

Evening comes and I call the other kitties in for the night. Patticake appears then dashes off. I call him repeatedly but he doesn't turn up again, and it looks like he is in for a cold night outside. I leave the porch light on, just in case, then settle down to read a new novel. The book sounds good and will hopefully divert my attention from my meandering pet. But I am still concerned.

Within a few pages of the book, a couple of characters coincidentally have a conversation about cats. They agree that the animals make themselves scarce when there is trouble and always do what they need to do to take care of themselves. This meaningful reminder about feline behavior is reassuring and I feel better immediately. It isn't long before Patticake comes around and then inside as usual for the night. And that we totally enclose a section of our yard so that this can't happen again!

Here's another instance of a book-delivered answer to an unintentional asking concerning a mental instead of physical issue:

July 2014, Salem: A story I've recently read starts me wondering about something. What is the single most important thing people can do to remain happy and in charge of the quality of their lives? Is this different for each person? Maybe not. I feel there is probably a common denominator that joyful, self-empowered people must share, regardless of how they personally express it.

I'm looking in the book section at a thrift store. An unknown book with the word "Choice" in its title catches my eye. I take a closer look, reading the book's description on the back cover. Then it hits me. Of course! "Choice" is the answer to my question. When we choose to think about the happier aspects of whatever is happening, we consistently feel good. And live the truth that the quality of our lives is always our own doing through those choices.

Divination

Before exploring how we can best request what we need and want in a personally tailored way, let's talk a minute about another traditional way of asking that we won't be considering here. Divination: methods of obtaining unknown knowledge by reading symbols and signs, according to fixed rules and interpretations.

Methods may involve interpreting signs or patterns in

nature or other things. Or they can involve choosing pre-determined symbols with their own fixed meanings. There are forms that work with words of particular books in which messages are searched for following set ways of asking. And there lies the rub – from my point of view – the fixed nature of the art.

Divination, which has been practiced around the world since the beginning of mankind, implies a message from the divine delivered through meaningful coincidences when fixed procedures are followed. Readings can certainly be helpful and clear. But limitations naturally occur when the vehicle of guidance and the meaning of its message are already fixed.

We can adapt a preset meaning as it may pertain to our own affairs with some success, and that's where divination may produce some remarkable insights, but why not go one step better? Allow the Universe to choose the perfect meaningful message for us through coincidental words, occurring wherever. No rules, no ritual, and no adaptation required. That being said, divination is sometimes right on with its message in spite of its constraints.

November 2012, Salem: I've been writing a book about antique jewelry for the last ten months. The topic is no longer as stimulating due to some source material I haven't been able to find and include. Besides, I keep thinking about synchronicity and the book I want to write about it. But not until this one is finished?

It doesn't seem right to just abandon my original project. And I know I will always be interested in synchronicity. So maybe to stay motivated with the jewelry topic, I should combine it with writing about coincidence? I decide to try divination to hopefully gain some insight.

Mark Thurston's book, *Synchronicity as Spiritual Guidance*, is what I choose to use. In it the author correlates answers of the ancient Asian oracle, the *I Ching*, with teachings of renowned psychic Edgar Cayce. My question is "Should I focus on both book ideas at the same time?"

I pose my question, then randomly open the book to the section of responses. My coincidentally chosen answer is "Seeking." "The search for truth," it begins, "is fraught with obstacles and disappointments. Sincere seeking means making choices along the way, and selecting one way at a crossroads means foreclosing another way. Even though mistakes and errors sometimes arise – even though gains along the way are offset by losses – keep to your search and the ideal that inspires it."

What a wonderful response! The answer is precisely right on. Choose one focus, one book to work on in my case, and let the other go. Keep investigating what intuitively feels right and true. I do just that, dropping the jewelry project and beginning to write about this book's fascinating subject.

Personal Intentional Asking

It seems the best way to benefit from the higher intelligence around us is to ask for it in our own way. We can strive to stay in the flow of life and receive its help that is always available. When we follow our intuition to personal ways of feeling good, then question, synchronicity occurs. The needed info or answers will appear. This will be the result whether we are looking for answers about simple things or matters more complex.

Of course, the nature of the cosmos is to spontaneously respond when we are concentrating on a question. So we don't really need to formally ask. But we do need to question in one way or another to receive its answering words. And be mentally receptive. A state of relaxed quiet without the static of negative thoughts seems to work best.

Getting into this state will be different for each of us. Every person has her or his own bag of tricks for feeling calm and serene. We probably know these activities that relax us, and gravitate to them from time to time. If not, a little thought about what we are doing during peaceful times will suffice. We can use these same things to put ourselves into a conducive mood for deliberate asking, turning to activities that help us relax.

It doesn't really matter what these activities are, as long as they work for us. Maybe we meditate or daydream or look at nature. Do crafts, play music, read books. We might find physical exertion the most relaxing – walking, dancing, gardening – whatever. Anything, really, that puts us in the zone is good. Of course, we might also simply tell ourselves to relax, take a deep breath or two, and be there. Whatever creates that physical calm.

May 2014, Salem: I am at the library, looking for a novel to read. It would be great to find one that has something to do with coincidence, I think to myself. Since author Deepak Chopra has written non-fiction on the subject, I decide to look at his novels. Maybe one of them will include it. A novel of his entitled *The Daughters of Joy* sounds vaguely familiar. I check its synopsis and think I may have already read it, or at least begun to. Then read a few paragraphs of the story that don't catch my attention. I start to reshelf the book.

As I do, the pages shift a bit, and I see that there is something inserted between them. Letting the pages fall open, I find the forgotten bookmark, a $1 bill. How funny! It feels like the Universe is humorously giving me a little gift to check out and read this book. The words, "In God We Trust" on the back side of the bill first catch my eye. And I realize I am being reminded to trust the force and flow with its energy through first impulses. I check out the book. And yes, synchronicity is involved in its tale.

When we decide to intentionally ask, there are unlimited ways to do it. Whatever feels right to us as we form and state our questions is our way. We might experiment with different variables when asking for what we need and want. Then note what feels best to us. Follow our own instincts and play with the process a while.

Staying flexible is important as we ask. We may change our mind about what or how we want to question mid-stream. Or do something totally different one time we ask than another. The key is to go for what spontaneously seems right at the moment.

The words we choose for our questions are significant. We need to use phrasing that feels good and clearly asks for what we want. This is pretty easy when we have a simple request, but a little harder with complex ones. We can play with the wording first, or jot it down, to get it just right.

We might phrase questions as an intent or as a request, "I would like guidance about..." or "please provide guidance about..." Or as a more general inquiry, "what do I need to be aware of concerning..." We can ask for a precise direction, "which way should I go on..." or maybe "what's best for me to do about..."

We can ask to receive a message as part of our question, "please send a message regarding..." or "I would like a message concerning..." or not. And we can also ask for a specific sign, "if (such and such) is right for me, I will see the word..." or "hear someone say..." etc. Or we even can specify timing as in, "if this is the answer, I will come across repeated information within a day."

Really, when it comes to asking the Universe, our options are wide open. The only rule of sorts is to make our question both clear and concise. We usually can best do this by focusing on one question at a time in a calm and relaxed moment. If that doesn't quite do the trick, there's always the option of repeating our question or requesting clarification about info received, later. As long as we first have asked.

August 2014, Salem: I am busy writing this chapter on asking. In the middle of my work I think that it would be interesting to experiment now, with just what I am writing about, to add to the chapter. I decide to ask about what's relevant, the way I normally do, by going over my question a few times then being alert for possible answers. So I do, mentally inquiring, what is the most important thing for me to know about asking for answers?

I proceed with my day, deliberately choosing to go a few places where words and phrases are plentiful, in case my experimental response is there. After some errands, I hit the used book store. I prowl all over the place for an hour or so, looking at fiction and nonfiction alike, as well as check out journals and cards and other wordy items for sale. But nothing jumps out at me and says, "Hey – here's your answer."

Later, I browse a craft supply store. I deliberately go over my question a few more times as I look through the aisles of paper, rubber stamps, stickers etc. But nothing is there for me either. It seems this is one of those times of no immediate answer, so I drop the experiment, consciously anyway.

Later in the evening, I start watching a television movie portrayed as a true historical tale. I'm not familiar with the film, and the actors' regional accents are a little hard to understand. But the story is charming and curious and compelling, and soon I am eagerly following along.

It takes place in an earlier time, and is about a couple who acquire evidence of otherworldly life. It also concerns a slew of other people who become involved in the events and their consequences. And, of course, as these stories often do, the concepts of belief versus disbelief, and fact versus fiction.

As the tale unfolds, the physical evidence is studied and discussed by an assortment of people, believers and non-believers alike. Eventually coming to the attention of – "Mr. So and So." Who? I think as he first appears. For his role in this story catches me completely off-guard. Oddly enough, right now I am reading a book which includes the same person, as well as issues of trust. I feel a little thrill run through me recognizing a sync in the making.

I watch the rest of the film and end up thoughtful. The story winds to some surprising conclusions. Naturally I am eager to get back to my book and check for its inclusion. Later I do, and the written account holds yet another sign.

I find that one person involved in the incidents experienced an uncanny coincidence. And felt that his role in the events was not chance, but arranged by a higher force. Reading this, another reference to *my* topic, is a confirmation for me. Most of all, I am struck by the different levels of trust among the participants. And there is my answer. The most important thing about asking the Universe is a willingness to believe enough to let its answering coincidences unfold.

Sometimes the impetus for a meaningful coincidence remains a mystery. We know something wonderful has happened, but it is a puzzle just who asked for the occurrence in the first place. The following sweet story holds such a secret.

July 2014, Salem: My friend Sophie leans forward in her

chair. "When I heard this story I got chills," she says, speaking of an experience that had been related to her. We are downtown having coffee. Knowing my bent for anything synchronistic, Sophie is excited to tell me her tale. And naturally I am just as eager to hear it.

"My friend May," she begins, "loves to bargain hunt. She finds all kinds of stuff at the secondhands including some real treasures. Once she even found a bracelet decorated with diamond chips in a shop's reject bin." Sophie relates that about five years ago, May found a notebook at the same place. It was a pretty little book with a colorful cover design. The inside was blank, but on the back was the full signature of a French woman's name. May bought the book, took it home, and set it on a table by the couch. She would use a piece of its paper from time to time, but mostly just enjoyed its beauty. Then something unusual happened.

"May's grandson was getting married," Sophie says. When the wedding announcement arrived she was struck by the young woman's name listed there. Why did this French name sound so familiar? She stood up to adjust the blinds at the window. At that moment a sunbeam shone down upon the journal and it came to her. The surnames on the two were the same!"

Sophie says that May decided to give her grandson's intended the pretty book at an upcoming shower. It just felt like the right thing to do for some reason or another. She wrapped it up with an accompanying note saying that this was an odd gift, but that she would explain the whole thing later.

She continues, "When the present was unwrapped at the shower, its recipient was astonished. 'That's my great grandmother's name written there! This must have belonged to her!' She told how the older woman had died just a few weeks before. Yet somehow, here was her personal book, now in her great granddaughter's hands via a near stranger." Uncanny.

So what really went on here? Whose asking actually prompted these events? And why? Was it May's desire to welcome the young woman into the fold that triggered her finding the book? Finding it – strangely – five years before? Or was it great grandmother's hope, from the other side, to bring the two families together. Someone sparked the stars to line up, that's for sure. But we'll probably never know who!

What needs to happen before helpful answers appear? Clear and concise asking. Then our willingness to be open and attentive to however they may come. After deliberately forming our questions, we can do things or go places to relax and be receptive. Or do nothing at all. Whatever feels right to us is just that, and we should follow along to life's wise and answering flow.

15

Recognizing Synchronicity

October 1962, Monmouth, OR: My sister Gayle tells me this touching story of recognizing meaningful words at a critical moment. "It was nearly midnight, and I was in a horrible mess. A freshman in college, I had come down with appendicitis and ended up in the hospital. It was an emergency situation, and permission had already been obtained for surgery. But mom and dad and you were still hours away, and I was among strangers – lying in a room waiting – and terribly afraid.

"A woman came in to keep another patient company. She talked to her a bit then noticed me. Smiling, she came over and introduced herself as Sue. 'Are you a student here?' she asked.

"'Yes', I replied, 'in elementary education. I'm going to be a teacher. But I guess I have to have this operation first.' My eyes welled up with tears.

"Sue sat down on the bed. 'What kind of operation are you having?' she gently asked. 'Does your family know?'

"I explained my condition and that the three of you were on your way. 'I have never had surgery before,' I confessed, 'and don't know anyone here.'

"Sue took up both of my hands. 'Well, now you know me,' she said softly. 'It will all be okay. And when you wake up your family will be here too. It really will be alright.'"

The reassuring words did the trick, and Gayle said she relaxed, feeling more comfortable and calm. She thanked Sue for talking with her and added a footnote: "You remind me so much of my Auntie Sis. She's my favorite aunt who always took good care of me when I when a kid visiting my cousins. And you know, you really look like her, too!'

"'Well, isn't that a coincidence!' Sue replied."

Gayle says she knew, somehow, that it was much more than that. "I never forgot Sue or the kindness she offered – just when I needed it most."

So how do we recognize synchronicity? Those words through which the creative force provides caring, direction, and answers to our questions? In some cases, like the incident just related, the message received is so con-spicuously pertinent to our circumstances that we can't help but notice. We read or hear something that we just know is meant for us. This often occurs when syncs result from unconscious concentration on an issue that's important to us. The coincidental answers are easy to spot and obviously personal.

When we become interested in the phenomena, how-ever, and begin deliberately asking for Universal help, we need to know how to notice its occurrence. Especially during those times when its appearance may be more subtle. Are there characteristics that coincidences exhibit no matter how large or small their concern? It seems that there are.

Before looking at some of these coincidental traits, we might consider how imagination ties into all of this. How do we know we aren't just making things up? How do we know a synchronicity is real and not just a product of our own minds? Seeing a link between our inner questioning and an outer message could be the result of imagination – seeing or hearing what we hope to.

Or selective observation. Looking for words in our environment that we have decided ahead of time will be the response. In spite of these risks, what it seems to get down to is being willing to suspend our doubts, expect an answer, and trust our own reactions to events. What we recognize as personally meaningful messages may be unnoticeable to others.

Intuition is our tool of discernment here. When we perceive synchronicity, it is our sixth sense that alerts us. Inner guidance draws our attention to what is right-on relevant. If we've deliberately questioned, we recognize the coincidental message as the answer to our query.

Alternately, if we are not currently looking for any particular info, our intuitions may be insights about most anything at all. Wisdom from a higher source, so to speak, instead of specific answers from the same. The Universe is ever sharing knowledge that may be beneficial or nurturing to us, as in this playful exhibit of nature.

December 2011, Salem: It is early morning and I am outside having coffee on the patio. Last night was cold and everything is frosty, though the sun beaming through is bright. I notice something I don't remember seeing before.

Tiny silver sparkles are dancing in the light. They lazily drift and swirl, capturing tints of color. I appreciate their show for a few minutes, then take a closer look. They turn out to be frozen bits of mist condensed on the roof above. There is an a-ha moment coupled with a quick feeling of truth. Magic, I think, genuine and just for show, surrounds us all. If we will only take the time to see!

Striking & Unique

One of the first traits that we will sometimes notice about synchronicities is that their messages are physically striking. Words conveying them stand out for us, whether read or heard. We will notice a word or phrase on a paper, book, sign, or whatever over others around it, or likewise, particular words spoken over other speech. It's as if the message calls, "Here I am, pay attention to me!"

Sometimes written words or the objects they are written upon can even look larger or brighter than their surroundings, and a similar thing can occur with spoken words. People and objects involved in the communication may seem to physically stand out in some way. Although we don't always notice this physical difference between the words of OUR messages and their surroundings, they usually manage to attract our attention in some way or another as distancing themselves from other distractions.

Synchronistic language sometimes is also unique. Words and phrases of messages from higher intelligence may be unusual or surprising. Information is communicated in an original way with written or spoken terms catching our attention with their uncommon or even bizarre nature. Once again, it seems to ensure that we notice.

Another way the words of coincidence may make an impression on us is through repetition. We may see the same written word or phrase in numerous locations in a short time. Or similarly, we may hear several people talking about the same subject, or using similar expressions repeatedly.

Words and phrases that we have seen or heard may linger in our minds as well, or repeat themselves over and over. Until we pay attention and recognize their worth. As with all "rules" of synchronicity, this doesn't happen every time. In fact, sometimes a single reading or hearing of the right words is completely adequate.

September 2014, Salem: As I begin working on this new chapter, I am again attracted to the idea of experimenting with its subject while writing about it. There's always more to learn about coincidence. Exploring the process of recognizing syncs while in the middle of relating past experiences of the same seems like a good way to do that. So I consider what I most want to know and focus on the question a bit. "What is the most important thing for me to know about recognizing synchronicity?"

I work a while on my writing then stop off at the mall to pick up a card and some gift wrap. The items I am planning to mail are irregularly shaped, so tissue paper might work best. The store has a fun selection of birthday prints in vibrant colors. I look at one, then another, and another, then go back to the first. I can't decide.

Another woman comes up and starts doing the same thing. She handles one pattern then a different one, then returns to the first. This hits me as funny and I kiddingly comment, "Very important decision, which pretty paper, isn't it?"

She laughs and replies, "And it probably doesn't really matter at all."

I sense a little sadness mixed in with her humor and quickly say, "but it does matter to us!" She smiles and nods her agreement. We each finish our selection then, and go our separate ways. I'm not even up to the checkout before feeling a subtle internal click. Ah, I think, the answer to my own question. I've just intuited and even vocalized the response aloud. We recognize synchronicities when their messages feel meaningful. What their words say MATTERS to us. And that is what is most important.

Meaningfulness

One of the most identifying traits of synchronicity is meaningfulness. Its communication to us is significant. This is the case whether we understand the intended message of a coincidence in a flash, or not until sometime later. We still know the event is important, whether in a small or momentous way.

Syncs are meaningful in several manners. First, they confirm the subject that is on our mind. Their words pertain to the same topic we have been thinking about; their messages to the focus of our thoughts.

Secondly, they relate to the exact aspect of this subject that concerns us. Messages convey precise, not simply relative information. Information pertaining to our questions or needs about a very particular thing.

Thirdly, they are timely to our situation. Messages respond to our circumstances at the most ideal time. Words we read or hear seemingly by chance answer our questions right as needed.

Lastly, they are composed of terms that make sense. Words we basically understand in what they say. At the same time their language often resonates deeper with us in some mysterious way. Even if we don't understand the message of an incident, we usually recognize its appearance. Through the multi levels of personal meanings that its words, by coincidence, portray.

Feeling

The second most conspicuous trait of synchronicity is feeling. We perceive meaningful coincidence through both our thoughts and our feelings. Intellectually, we note its significance, emotionally we sense its spirit. When we recognize an event as a meaningful coincidence there usually is an instinctive physical and emotional response as well as a mental knowing.

We may experience goose bumps, chills or even a pounding heart, along with the feelings of energy and surprise. Or amazement leading to spontaneous joy. For we sense that we are linked to something far bigger and wiser than ourselves. Something that is caring and sharing of the information we seek.

This feeling of aliveness and connection to a higher power seems to be there whenever we clearly recognize a coincidence, whether or not we understand its message. We feel the force of being in sync with the world even if not sure what it is telling us. Take for example the puzzling yet fun feel that surrounds this cluster coincidence.

March 2013, Salem: Eric tells me he just learned the last name of our neighbors across the street is Moore. My maiden name is Moore. Although it is a fairly common surname, I have rarely come into contact with more than an occasional Moore (no pun intended), in my life, until recently.

It started with a neighbor who lived next door at our previous residence. His last name was Moore, and we became friends. Later, we moved to our current house and met the new Moores who also live next door. Now we have learned about the additional Moores living across the street and I am starting to pay attention.

A few weeks go by when Deidre tells me of a helpful coincidence concerning the owner of a vintage clothing shop – also named Moore, I don't know what all this is about, but there is *something* afoot. I can feel it. A message of some sort trying to get through as we Moores start to add up!

Sometimes, as noted, we definitely perceive a synchronicity, but have no idea of its meaning. We have a strong sense or a subtle recognition that coincidental words hold meaning for us, we just don't know how. If we are alert to what is happening, and note the particulars, our uncertainty will often disappear. Down the road the message received is apt to be perfectly clear.

The following incident falls into this category. Both Eric and the other bicyclist it involves were left with an easy yet insistent knowing that what transpired held a purpose. Perhaps by now the other guy has a good idea what the events were saying to him. Eric explains.

March 2013, Salem: "I had been wanting a particular type of bicycle pump. I checked out bargain places and found one for a couple dollars at a new thrift store in town. It was a great buy, though I still needed a small part used to attach it to the bike. I looked at an online classifieds, and found the exact little part that I needed at a cheap price. So I arranged the sale and went to pick it up.

"When I got there, the two of us talked shop, exchanging bicycling stories. One the seller shared was particularly interesting. It seems that not long before he had seen a bike for sale like one he had owned many years before. It brought up fond memories and he decided he would like to own one again – to buy this one for fun. So he arranged the purchase.

"When he went to pick up the bicycle, and saw it in person, he was astounded. This bike wasn't just similar to his old one, but was identical. In fact it was, coincidentally, the very same bike that he had owned all those years before!"

Our recognition of synchronicity varies in intensity. We realize coincidental words are answers just for us in different degrees. Sometimes pertinent words arrive with a strong and forceful feel as if determined to catch our attention. Other times they feel much lighter. Whether we perceive them as loud shouts or as subtle whispers doesn't really matter, we perceive them either way. And that recognition is the first step to understanding their message.

Our noticing of the intuitions leading up to syncs varies in intensity too. Those inner prompts that urge us to go somewhere or to do something that we hadn't considered or planned. These promptings can range from feeling like a powerful push to a soft and gentle nudge, or anything in between, and serve to get us into place to experience our incidents. Personally, I am often guided to information by subtle rather than strong intuitions that gently guide me to where the answers are. Like this.

September 2014, Salem: I email Deidre, mentioning a mystery novel I have just read and thoroughly enjoyed. She responds that my description sounds like the writing of another author, a favorite of hers. I jot down a book she recommends and reserve it online.

At the library, I pick up the book then feel an urge to check out the author's other works. I don't know why; I am certainly not short of reading material and currently am in the middle of reading several books. But I follow the feeling, looking her up on the computer catalog and finding about a dozen other titles she has written.

One, about her personal experiences as a novelist, catches my eye. I keep rereading its brief synopsis. which though sounding pretty routine, entices me for some reason. So I give in and track down the book. Pulling if off the shelf, I open it at random to scan a few paragraphs. What I read draws me right in. The author is discussing meaningful coincidence and some experiences with it – right up my alley.

16

Understanding Coincidence

Once we have recognized something as a meaningful coincidence, the real fun begins. Just what is our personal message from the Universe? Whether we've consciously asked a question of higher forces or unconsciously done so doesn't matter. Now we want to know what it means. As already explored, language means different things to different people. Individual words and phrases hold personal associations as well as standard meanings. Because the words we use communicate what is real for us, the Universe often uses these same terms to talk to us. Relay the shades of meaning we personally employ.

Synchronistic words are also power words as needed. Terms with strong undertones of feeling that can change our points of view. Messages coincidentally read or heard can shift perceptions, serving as powerful personal catalysts. Of course, some syncs are simple answers we understand immediately, using standard terms. Others are more complex, using words as symbols with layers of meaning and tone. Whether simple or complex in nature, our understanding of coincidence often varies in many ways.

Immediate or Gradual

Our understanding of a synchronicity may be instantaneous or progressive, our awareness of its meaning all at once or in degrees. We may immediately understand its message or come to comprehend it sometime later on.

Simple coincidental messages often answer simple questions. Common everyday terms are used to respond to what is asked. Multiple meaning personal words are usually not needed to convey their necessary facts or information. These types of syncs are most likely to be instantly and completely understood when received.

October 2014, Salem: I am in an import store browsing for Christmas gift ideas. It's an enjoyable place to shop, with all its varied wares. I especially like finding unusual items that are decorative and not readily available elsewhere.

I come across a unique doormat. It is multicolored and made from recycled flip flops. What a fun gift this would be for my son Jason! Besides, I noticed when last at his apartment that his doormat looked pretty worn.

The only drawback is the item's coloring. Half of its appeal is the rainbow of brightly colored parts that make it up. But Jason is red-green colorblind, and sees some tones as unattractive shades if at all. So I usually buy him things in single colors that I know he can see.

I put the mat down on the floor to take a better look at it. A woman browsing nearby glances over. I make some comment about how fun the mat is, but that I am not sure how my partially colorblind son would see it. "Well," she says smiling, "it happens that I am colorblind, too, and I can tell you that lots of these colors really stand out!"

"Thank you so much!" I say. And thank you – *big U* – for providing the perfect person to so quickly answer my question. Especially considering that only about one out of two hundred women are colorblind and qualified to do so!

Synchronicities pertaining to more complicated issues are apt to convey similarly more involved answers. Words and phrases of their messages include those with personal associations. Certain terms in these messages allow us to comprehend a symbolic meaning as well as a literal one. They are able to stand for several shades of meaning unique to ourselves.

These complex coincidences are more likely to be gradually understood. Although insight of their entire meaning may intuitively come in a flash, it often does not. Many times a basic understanding of the message comes quickly with additional facets of meaning later on. It seems we are given precisely the information we need right then, with more supplied incrementally as required. Like this:

March 2011, Salem: I am at the library browsing the stacks. In a novel I find one of my favorite things, a forgotten bookmark. This one is a handwritten note on a sheet from a doctor's prescription pad. It says, "Hotel at the Corner of Bitter & Sweet," and I recognize the wording as the title of a current novel I really know nothing about.

It's a catchy title, and I keep running over the words as I look for reading material. "Hotel at the Corner of Bitter and Sweet," seems to me to symbolically refer to living temporarily (hotel) at both a bad feeling (bitter) and a good feeling (sweet) place. With the reality determined by which street one chooses as her or his address. The concept the wording brings up for me is suddenly recognizable as the answer to a question I've been pondering lately – what thought can a person live by to feel good, no matter what is happening? CHOOSE to reside in the best feeling place.

As I share the account of this incident right now, I am struck by another level of meaning I somehow missed before. The RX pad. I asked how we can feel good consistently, and the Universe suggested its remedy on a physical sheet of paper used for the same purpose in everyday life.

In this case, however, the prescription seems to have been offered by a most clever guide intent on my noticing and understanding. I do, and will remember just what the wise doctor coincidentally ordered. And another coincidence with gradually expanded meaning:

April 2013, Salem: I've been thinking about lifepaths and the writing of this book It feels so right for me to do this now, even though the writing part of the project can be challenging. As opposed to the research and experimentation – always exciting.

I stop in at a thrift store to browse and naturally end up in the books section. Quickly I zero in on an interesting title unfamiliar to me, *The Reinchantment of Everyday Life* and randomly open the book to a chapter on *Books and Calligraphy*. I am drawn to a paragraph in which author Thomas Moore explores his ideas about the enchantment of writing and the power of words.

His thoughts and his word-play speak straight to me. For my study of synchronicity is full of encounters with this mysterious force. The key to joyful writing, I realize, is to share how the discoveries of magic have enchanted me. And that is what I am trying to do.

As I later record this incident in my journal, I am struck by another of its facets. Recurring words that were also used in the previously described experience of a few months before, through the billboard for the *Enchanted Forest*. That coincidental answer addressed basically the same theme of maintaining enjoyable writing. And like the earlier message, this second one relayed that sharing the most personally enchanting encounters with synchronicity is the thing to do.

If we've kept track of our synchronicities, writing down what happened and how we felt to the best of our recollections, we are more likely to notice these highlighted terms, as well as figure out their message. With me, anyway, it often takes several incidents communicating the same important point before I finally get it.

Surprising or Unexpected

Synchronistic messages may be surprising. Their meanings may astonish, even startle us. In addition to surprising messages, their methods of arrival or other elements may be unexpected as well.

Sometimes coincidences that disclose their meanings gradually surprise us with their complexity. We are amazed by the breadth and depth of their meanings. As we figure out what they are saying to us, our surprise is often followed by flashes of intuitive insight.

Some of the most surprising coincidences use metaphorical language. Words of common things that also describe the abstract. What startles us is the unexpectedness of the literary device that so cleverly conveys our answers, and helps us understand a concept in a deeper way.

It's as if by speaking to us symbolically the Universe is more likely to be heard. And then to be understood. By comparing the familiar with what is not we can usually make sense of the coincidence and its multi-layered message for us.

For example, the incident related earlier concerning the unfavorably named street sign I came upon while questioning, exhibited this phenomena. At the time, I clearly recognized the importance of the coincidence, but not its message. Seeing this tangible sign bearing the same unusual name as someone whose personality I was discussing right then was downright disconcerting. I reluctantly guessed it confirmed that we shared some troubling traits. Still, that conclusion didn't feel right in some intuitive way. I just wasn't sure how.

The episode served nicely, though, to shine a light on my own actions. I was reminded how potent our own words to others can be. Though not certain what it meant for me to see the sign at that moment, I did know it was significant. And hoped to understand more later.

And that is what happened. I don't know when or how, but one day I was surprised to remember the event in a totally different way. This time the offending street sign of Ms. Such & Such was recognized as representing a *crossroad* near the street I was currently using. Literally I could choose to go down that road or not. And symbolically, options were wide open. I could pass that unpleasant byway of behavior completely and stay on the better course. The decision was entirely mine. This time I got it.

On a lighter note, the surprise element is often in the workings of syncs relating to less serious matters too. Sometimes the pinpoint timing or unexpected delivery method used to convey info we want is astounding. And lots of fun. The following story was shared with me via email by my long-time friend Heather.

October 2014, Medford, OR: "Yesterday I needed to buy some supplies at the fabric store," Heather begins. "After doing my shopping, I decided to run into the discount store next door, just for the heck of it. And when I did, there hanging on a rack was the most beautiful dress in black and cerulean blue. I was smitten – again.

"What happened was this. Months ago I had been shopping for a special dress at a local department store. I found one, the same cap sleeve, blue and black swing dress, in just my size. Only problem was that it cost too much. I tried it on anyway, and luckily it was a little too tight, so I wasn't tempted to buy it. But it sure was a pretty thing!

"Now here was the exact same dress hanging in front of me in the next larger size. With a much lower price tag, too. I tried it on, naturally, and it fit well. So I bought it! The only hitch was that it didn't seem to have a fabric content or cleaning instructions tag. Even so, it was a bargain. I really wasn't planning to buy another dress right now, but I couldn't pass up the deal.

"Right now as I was writing this email to you about the incident, an Internet ad for a clothing site popped up. On a whim I clicked on their section of dresses. Surprisingly a picture of my new dress with its detailed description just appeared. Now my questions about the dress's fabric and care have been answered, too!"

Puzzling or Undecipherable

Coincidental answers are sometimes puzzling. We may recognize the significance of their words but be mystified by their overall meanings. Or we may understand part of their messages for us but be confused by other parts, finding them vague and uncertain. There are a few common causes for these cases of undecipherable syncs, and things we can do to sometimes clear thing up.

Often if we are just patient, our understanding of the force's coincidental responses will come. There will be a gradual comprehension of the message, hours, days, or even months later. In hindsight we will be able to look at the incident anew and easily intuit what it meant for us then and now.

If not, and it is an answer to a question still important

to us, it is likely to repeat again. Through a different arrangement of coincidentally delivered words. And we always can ASK for clarification, or for another sign entirely, with the same message for us. The Universe aims to please.

We also can spend some time with self-analysis techniques of various kinds. When our intellect quiets down, our intuition may be heard with its messages. Using methods such as these often allows us to suddenly understand the answer to a puzzling coincidence.

No Answer

There are times when the response we receive from a deliberately asked question is no answer at all. We are focused on our need but nothing happens to provide the information that we seek. Though there certainly isn't any way to know for sure what's going on in these cases, a few types of scenarios are often in play.

It may be one of those occasions we have explored when our understanding of a message will occur in stages. In these instances, the initial answer made up of coincidental words is still forthcoming. If we are patient and open, the meaning of the incident will gradually unfold.

Or it may be that no answer is our answer, meaning simply to wait. Perhaps circumstances are not yet ready to provide us with what we need. We can be sure, however, that the Universe will orchestrate objects, people, or events to offer us the best answer, when the time is right. If we can hold off awhile.

It also may be that we are personally not ready to receive an answer to our question. Perhaps our mental or physical state needs to change first. Then again, to have some tolerance for delay or even confusion about the whole thing may be the meaning itself, until more apparent answers come.

Or, finally, receiving no answer to our deliberate questioning may be a result of our inexperience. Maybe we just didn't recognize the message that came. Until we can trust that the phenomena of synchronicity is valid and always available, our doubts can interfere. It's that old adage about having happen or not happen, what we expect or don't expect, to occur in our lives. But we can learn.

Questions for Understanding

Though the messages of some synchronicities may be immediate or gradual, simple or complex, surprising or even undecipherable; we somehow know when they are personally important. These chance events simply *feel* significant to us. If we are willing to explore their mystery, we will come to understand their meaning.

Our challenge is to dig deeper when necessary to make sense of their language. Look below the surface to comprehend their coincidental words. We really are the only ones who can do this – read the meaning of our synchronicities' terms. But there are some basic questions that can help us along.

Realizing that there's a cosmic force available right now to respond to our questions is exhilarating. Meaning that the answers to secrets of the Universe as well as simple inquiries are always there. In light of this offer of higher wisdom, it's good to remember our gratitude. An attitude of appreciation along with anticipation of adventure is a most helpful approach.

When the understanding of a sync is not forthcoming, we often automatically ask ourselves what we had been thinking about. Were our thoughts before the coincidence focused on a particular issue or concern? Had we been deliberately looking for an answer to a question or the solution to a problem? This is apt to be the most helpful train of thought towards eventual understanding.

Since coincidences come in response to our immediate concerns, it is essential to determine just what they've been. What question has been most on our minds? Or looking at it another way – what were the conditions surrounding its occurrence, and what were we thinking about them? These lines of inquiry are likely to help us determine what the synchronicity addressed.

A second basic question for self-understanding pertains to a coincidence's form. Does it wording feel factual or figurative? Is the message a metaphor? Are its words used in a non-exact way to refer to something they do not usually apply to? Coincidental words used figuratively can sometimes be more meaningful to us than literal ones. Or offer us more levels of insight.

Sometimes Universal answers combine metaphorical and literal words, or a mixture of terms with non-literary symbols thrown in as well. I tend to think of these jumbles as the apparent best way to get a message through to us that we have somehow been missing. The answer is conveyed in a couple different ways to make sure we get it. These mixed symbol messages can be both powerful and reassuring.

November 2014, Salem: It is evening and I am stewing about something I need to do tomorrow. It is something important, and I know it is necessary for me to do. But certainly no fun. In fact, I've been wondering if I can successfully get through the whole thing at all.

I'm restless and don't feel like doing any of my normal evening activities. I get a little urge to play cards, though not really a games person, and maybe only mess around with a deck a couple times a year. But I follow it, setting up the layout for a game of Solitaire. The cards I draw are good from the start. All four aces quickly emerge then their successions of suit cards. Within a few minutes all cards are up and I have won the game.

This is fun, and I don't feel like ruining my streak with a second game. The words "dealt a good hand" run through my mind. That's what I want for tomorrow, to be dealt a good hand. Experience good luck of the draw. It feels most likely now. A bit later I come across the phrase "you pass the test" in some reading material, and the words seem to stand out to me and reinforce the message.

Of course, things fall smoothly into place the next day – very much like a winning hand of Solitaire or acing a personal challenge.

When working with basic questions to understand a coincidence, we will notice its familiar terms. Personal language has been used to catch our attention as well as pertinently speak. What better way to share information than through our own favorite words and phrases. The Universe always chooses the very best jargon for its private messages to us. Even if the message is metaphorical, it will usually consist of language we are partial to. Serving to ensure we grasp the full meaning of its words. It seems our personal vocabulary is essential to a meaningful coincidence, no matter how complex its meaning.

In addition to keeping a record of experiences, it is advantageous for us to track our symbolic lexicon. We will find that certain words, objects, or images repeatedly appear in our lives. When they do, we intuitively recognize them as holding multiple meanings for us; standing for more than one thing. Often these personal symbols also appear in our dreams, signifying something of conse-quence. Wherever they appear, paying attention to them is the key. For through outer signs or inner images the Universe sends its messages.

When it comes to synchronicity, perhaps the final test of accurate understanding is our feelings. Does our pro-posed meaning of a coincidence seem to click? Does this answer, delivered in personal jargon feel both right and true? If so, then we've got it. Now and then though something more is needed to reach this understanding...

December 2014, Salem: More coincidences crop us as I'm

working on this chapter. As is normal when I write, the current section's subject is often in the back of my mind throughout the period and during other activities. For some reason, though, I start focusing on a totally different subject, too – another bunch of old letters.

I had come across this cache a few weeks before. The letters were for sale in a downtown shop, stored in a small box at the back of the store. From my first glance, there had looked to be quite a number. But I hadn't taken time then to really look them over, or even think about them much, until now.

Those old letters. A flash comes to mind of lost ancestors. As in relatives lost through the busyness of time. Past generations of families casually and carelessly forgotten. I start imagining that these very notes may be the records of such people, unremembered and sadly misplaced.

The fact of their private letters laying there in the shop really bothers me. Letters undoubtedly full of personal sentiment and thought. But what if the identity of the authors could be determined along with descendants? Surely genealogists would love to get to know these new family members.

I am really getting carried away with my fantasies here. Who knows what the letters are even about or their intended recipients? Let alone the nature of their authors. After all, they are just a bunch of faded old letters, aren't they? Still, a part of me won't let it go and seems to need to know if *these* letter people have been forgotten.

I head down to the shop intent on getting a better look at the papers. Once there I find a table and chair and began doing just that. I see that some of the letters are still in their original opened envelopes, postmarked from the late 1800s. They were sent from the Midwestern states to several different people. I quickly realize that I want to read every single one of them in my own time and space. So I buy the whole boxful.

Later at home, I start by counting them and find more than 60 letters! There looks to maybe some other paper items tucked into a few envelopes as well. I see that many of the letters were written between the same couple, so begin my reading there and am quickly pulled back into their sentimental tale.

"Addie" and "Dan" were young newlyweds in the middle 1890s. They had married in a tiny corner town of Kansas and set up housekeeping for a while. Their life together was interrupted, however, and they were forced apart – Addie stayed in Kansas and Dan went to Nebraska. He found work there and saved hard for a place of their own.

The letters crisscrossed the states, sharing sweet sentiments and newsy bits, recording young lives. They did see each other occasionally, there were reunions carefully planned and enjoyed. But severe weather and eldercare kept them apart many long months of the year.

And then came "Belle." The "precious Christmas present" arrived in the middle of the holidays, and Addie and Dan were smitten. Letters from Mama to Papa, and those from Papa to Mama now included things Baby. Plus more hopes and plans for togetherness. And then they stopped. There were no more letters between the couple, and I can't help wonder – did they make it?

I take a break from my reading to go online. Searching, I quickly come up with an auction listing that includes their names. Seems someone in Georgia just happens to have for sale an original copy of the couple's marriage announcement right now. Strange.

Later, I go through the letters again checking for dates. I find a few in the early 1900s addressed to them both as a couple. They made it! Together again. There was a jump of a few more years, then daughter Belle started receiving letters in a totally different place – California. Then there were references to her parents, and I find that the family relocated to the much warmer climate of Los Angeles.

Belle grew up and started a career, and her parents eventually moved to Oregon in the 1930s. To southern Oregon more precisely, to *Grants Pass.* When I see the first reference to the place it surprises me, as this, coincidentally, is my hometown. And furthermore, it turns out that their neighborhood was the very same one where I grew up! Stranger yet.

Did I meet descendants of this family when I was a kid? Maybe so. And does my finding of the letters, right now, serve as a link in someone else's synchronicity? Time, as they say, will tell. I'll have to do some serious searching to find out if these people from the past have family looking for them!

17

Extra Helps for Understanding Coincidence

There are times when we get stuck – understanding-wise. A synchronicity has happened that we know is meaningful, but we just don't get its message. We have thought some about it yet still don't understand its words. How then can we crack the code of an extra confusing coincidence? Various techniques used in dream analysis and other inner work may help.

Syncs often speak to us metaphorically, as do dreams. Both are apt to use words with multi-meaning levels. It seems the coincidences we find most puzzling often are complex with several things to say. With a little self-analysis though, we can usually hear their messages.

From an assortment of techniques that may be helpful, I am partial to a few. These methods can quickly clarify some of our most puzzling incidents. My favorite techniques have been very helpful personally in understanding coincidence – and may be to you as well.

Word Association
A long used method for self-understanding, word association can reveal our personal concepts and links. For

instance, what does the sight or sound of a particular word bring to our mind? What other words or meanings do we quickly think of when considering these words? Our answers offer clues to understanding a coincidental message.

I decide to try the method with my many Moores experiences. So I begin by writing "MOORE" on the top of a piece of paper. Then I list as many single words and phrases as I can that quickly come to mind, without thinking about what I am writing.

What emerges is this: "more, many, numerous, Scots, Scottish, heather, surprising, number, scattered, everywhere, connected, connection, tied together, strings, more people tied together though apart." An image pops up, too, of some kind of map with locations marked by pins that are connected by string. How strange. I'm not sure where this is heading at all. Maybe another technique will clarify things.

Free Flow Writing

Also called "stream of consciousness writing," this technique is said to be helpful in uncovering our true thoughts and feelings. By starting with a chosen subject in mind, then writing fluidly in a continual non-thinking flow, we are able to bypass our conscious critic. And come up with what we truly feel. That's the concept anyway. I have had good luck with the method various times, so am anxious to apply it to my many Moores conundrum.

So I begin. Without considering what I might put down,

I just start writing phrases quickly that flow easily from my pen. After awhile, when nothing more comes, I go back and read what I have written finding this: "Moores. Mores. Many manners, many people. All different, but all the same. Connected by common desires and values inside, though different on the outside. Not always what they seem. We are connected more than we know. In more ways than we think. Not so different after all. Somehow tied together even when we think we are so far apart."

This is a total surprise! Not at all what I expected to come up with, but clearly mirrors ideas from the word associations. I did think it was strange when multiple Moores first started popping up. Though a common surname, I had come across few other people similarly names. Then as more Moores coincidentally appeared my antennae perked up. Something of significance was happening.

Now I mentally form the question, is the message that we are all more alike than we think? Connected in some hidden ways? I would welcome confirmation if this is the meaning of my expanding circle of Moores through another meaningful coincidence.

Confirmation Request

We always can ask the Universe for a repeat performance, request another message to validate what we've come up with so far. These confirmations often seem to occur quickly and clearly mirror the message of the first. If nothing happens. the best thing to do may be to put the whole thing aside and be open to a different meaning. In this case something new is apt to occur when the timing is right.

A few days after my confirmation request, I receive an email from my friend Heather. She is a long-time acquaintance; in fact, we have been friends since junior high school. And Heather is another person I know that really loves working on genealogy.

In fact, she enjoys climbing family trees so much that when she gets stuck on a branch of her own tree, she some-times works on mine – and often comes up with some amazing finds. This time she writes to say that she signed up for a new online program. And had been experimenting with it by plugging in various names of ancestors. And also working with one of my tougher lines as well – you may have guessed it – the Moores.

When she did, what happened next was a big surprise. As she discovered lineage going back further than we previously knew, some facts sounded awfully familiar. Weren't some of her *own* ancestors similarly named and living in those same places? More checking proved this was so – she and I were related! Common ancestors generations back had made us eighth cousins, in fact. Yet oddly, although we had grown up in the same town, become good and lasting friends, we had never known it.

When I read her note, I can't help but notice the repeat theme of hidden connections. Brought to me once again through a family of Moores. With Heather's help, of course, as the deliverer of a message that is becoming more clear to me with each relevant coincidence. But why now? The reason these coincidences are currently happening is a puzzle to me – or is it? Some as yet unclear ideas seem to be trying to get through. Maybe sleeping on it will trigger some sure-feeling insights.

Dream Requests

Another way we can receive higher guidance is through a dream. Our nighttime images can answer or confirm. We can inwardly pose our question before sleep and look for a response in the morning. Often our dreams will comply. I do this, thinking about the coincidences that have occurred concerning the Moores, plus word association and free flow writing results.

I awake remembering the following dream.

I am attending a large gathering, a genealogical conference of some kind. There is a lot of activity going on; people are talking and milling around, attending classes and lectures. I stand on the sidelines watching, dressed in PJ's and my robe. My son Jason comes up and stands beside me, also in his robe.

Thinking about the dream, a few things come to mind. First, is the setting of a family history gathering. Secondly, the way that I am dressed, symbolizing my unpreparedness for the event. There is a feeling of simply being an observer instead of one of those involved in the activities. After all, I'm still dressed in my robe! Then there's Jason's outfit, obviously similar to mine. This dream is NOT about actively climbing our tree.

Meditation Requests

We can also turn to traditional meditation for help in understanding coincidences. Consider their merit and meaning from that place of inner peace. From there insights may come to clarify answers or confirm our ideas. Puzzling words may be easily explained. Going within through the practice of meditation can be very helpful.

As a final technique for gaining understanding of the many Moores incidents, I sit quietly a few minutes and relax. Once in the zone, I mentally ask the same questions as before, plus my interpretation so far. Is the message of these incidents that we are somehow connected? All linked at some level or another?

I wait to see what may come, then feel a sense of affirmation with these words: "Yes, connected. Separate yet together, unique yet the same." Okay, I think, I get it now. Understand what these reminders have been all about. It seems I have learned something new that maybe, I once already knew? This feels true.

18

Responding to Synchronicity

Once we've experienced an intuition regarding our need, it is time to act. To follow up on the help we've been given. Without our response – inner, outer, or a combination of both – the coincidental answer on its way to us will be lost. We've got to do our part.

Our response may be quick or it may be slow, carried out after some deliberate thought. And, of course, can pertain to any level of seriousness, need or want-wise. But we must respond to our inner prompts to receive the higher help.

Quick Responses

Sometimes taking action on our intuitions is a given. We have a minor dilemma and need some help right now! When an idea comes through our intuition, we don't dally around thinking about it, but head out in the direction it points, looking for a solution.

A good example of this kind of sync concerns missing things. Items lost or misplaced in our everyday affairs. These often are common objects playing a necessary part in a current incident, a sometimes maddeningly necessary role. If we're aware of our inner promptings, coincidence will help us find them.

My cousin Toni beautifully describes this process in her take on the phenomena: "To me 'coincidences' are sign posts, pointing to God. 'Look up, I'm here and completely interested in YOU!' I've lost things (tiny things), and 'asked,' and been sent to where I've lost them (the mud in a parking lot of an antiques store in Vancouver, a spot in the grass on the east side of my house – weird stuff)."

She continues, "My sister Mandy, who for the most part has a tendency to be skeptical, relayed to me that she lost her keys somewhere in a giant junk store and searched the whole place, and then "asked," and saw them in a place she had already looked, only *above* her head in a spot with a beam of light shining on it! I expect it could all be explained away – except for those of us these things have happened to and know differently."

Exactly. And these answers don't always concern minor problems either. Sometimes our quick response to inner or outer messages concerns major or even life-threatening situations. Toni goes on, "I fell asleep in my van driving back one night from work and was awakened by a hard slug in the back (while my back was up against the seat), just as I was veering off into the water." Amazing!

This story reminds me of an uncanny personal driving incident. Back in the day when my friend Vivian and I were both booksellers, we often took buying trips to nearby town. These were fun and enjoyable times, full of shop talk, girlfriend, camaraderie, and the chance to discover some great books. But one such outing included an event that wasn't so pleasant.

November 2003, Oregon: We are on the highway, a busy stretch situated between Salem and Independence, our destination town. Viv is driving us in her van. On the road in front of us is a good-sized delivery truck full of lumber. As we ride along, busily discussing our plans for the day, I suddenly hear a mental voice shout out, "Change lanes now!"

The command is so insistent that I don't stop to analyze these words or their origin, just repeat them verbatim to my friend. She senses the urgency and clarity of the message and instantly follows directions. Then we both watch in shock as big, long boards begin flipping out of the truck onto the other lane.

After a few moments, we look back, and thankfully see other cars with more visual warning getting around the wood safely. But we both know our case was different. Without the Universal help, we wouldn't have been so lucky.

Our quick actions can be the best response to prompts concerning minor desires as well. Items we want to obtain or circumstances we want to occur. When we intuitively receive a suggestion concerning our problem, moving on it fast is often what is best.

As in the incident already related of Deidre and the old jewelry. She had ended up with a collection of pieces she wanted to sell quickly, fairly and without hassle. So when she happened to notice the sign for a new vintage clothing shop and had a flash – maybe *they* would be interested in the collection – she acted on it immediately. She found out that yes, the owner was very much interested. Seeing that her store, coincidentally, had just been robbed of one thing only, its jewelry. Or take this example of necessary, quick response, also by Deidre, to fill a pressing need:

April 2013, Corrales, NM: She relates, "I was really concerned about finding a provider who would take 'X' insurance, that offers medical coverage for spouses of disabled vets. No one in Salem, when we lived there, had accepted it. I was in the process of wading through the options, all of them expensive, when a person's not old enough for Medicare. At that point, my daughter intervened.

"She eagerly told me that she had seen an ad for a brand new facility affiliated with the University of New Mexico, that happened to have been built just up the road from Corrales. I called them immediately, and they made my day by saying something like, 'Of course we take 'X'! Easy as pie.

"Even better is the fact that Adam qualified for care in the same system, and voila, started getting super care for a condition he experienced after our move here, at one of their other centers. So it's been a long series of coincidences that, I think, have been directed by the Universe!"

Slow Responses

Although we usually must respond to our inner voice in order to trigger synchronicities, fast responses are not always needed. Sometimes slower reactions are what's called for. These are likely to be times when the Universe offers some guidance that coincidentally leads to a partial answer, or what seems like it anyway, at the time.

In these instances, we recognize its importance but don't understand the whole message. It appears we are given just the amount of information that we can use at the moment in these more complex situations. With more provided, coincidentally of course, after we respond.

Taking some kind of steps based on the guidance we've been given seems to be the key to receiving more help. Even if we're not sure what we're doing. Seeing and trusting the magic of the process. Being willing to make a decision or physically act on the message received so far.

Then watching for another. When we do this we are seldom disappointed as more info will be coincidentally provided, or confirmation given to lead us to our goal. The following is an example of this kind of incident, a synchronistic work in progress.

April 2013, Salem: Eric and I would like to move from Salem in a few years, and would like to decide the location now. We are considering the areas of Portland, here in the Willamette Valley; Grants Pass, in southern Oregon; and Santa Rosa, in central coastal California.

Each area offers some of what's important to us – sunnier, warmer climate, proximity to Jason, good libraries, bookstores, and natural food stores – but not all. It's like comparing apples and oranges and we're going round and round.

I put a request out to the Universe for information we most need to know. Immediately I receive an email from Heather who lives in southern Oregon. She writes of the problems the local libraries are having and the possibility of their closing due to lack of funding.

What a clear message for us! If this kind of problem continues in the area, we will not consider living there. Access to a large and dependable source of books and reading material is just too important. For us it would be the deciding factor to drop the region from our group of new home possibilities.

Of course, my friend had no idea when she wrote that she was providing an answer to my request. Her note just shared a situation that happened to be currently significant. Seems to be one of those complex issues that may involve multiple prompts leading to what's timely and meaningful, if I do my part by responding when led.

Intuitions followed by synchronicities followed by more intuitions etc. That often is the scenario when we act on our inner voice. When focusing on complex needs, our questioning is answered through the messages of meaningful coincidence.

Take my experience with the second cache of old letters bought from the antiques shop. That turned out to be the correspondence of that 1890s couple, unhappily living apart in Kansas and Nebraska. As I read their story, intimately recorded in personal letters between themselves and others, I was glad to find they were finally able to reunite and move to the warmer climate they craved in California.

Then I was utterly surprised to find them relocating again, a couple decades later to Oregon and my old hometown of Grants Pass. When further study of the letters and mailing addresses disclosed their final residence (as far as I could tell) to not only have been Grants Pass, but my old neighborhood as well, I really took notice.

So what is next? I put the letters away some months ago with the thought of someday reuniting them with their descendants. And then pretty much forgot about them. Until now, with the writing of this chapter, when they're once again on my mind with the desire to do something or other.

I'm not exactly sure what, but am imagining internet forums where researchers exchange information about lost and found ancestors. So maybe that's where I'll start by posting the discovery of the letters and the facts of their folks. Take that first step and then see what comes next. Who knows what answer I may provide for a family historian online – or vice versa.

19

Transformation Through Coincidence

Perhaps the greatest gift of synchronicity is its power to transform. Coincidence offers us the grand possibility of positive change. Whether our changes are small and simple, or big and complex, the potential to become or do something different is always there. Something more in alignment with what's true and real for us.

Meaningful coincidence can alter our inner worlds and the very ways we think and feel. They can offer us ideas that affect existing beliefs or create new ones. Our outer worlds may be changed as well, their circumstances; the things we do. Through messages of words we intuitively understand, syncs share their wisdom. Through happenchance answers they lead to different paths. Then encourage us to follow them.

For me, transformations are usually simple. Or seem so, at first anyway. They often go like this. A coincidence happens that is especially meaningful. It changes me in some small way then begins to snowball and snowball, nudging me to a completely different spot that where I started! Three important concepts about meaningful coincidence and life have personally evolved.

Knowing: From an initial suspicion that the phenomena probably existed, I've moved to a place of belief. For me, curiosity became certainty. My experiences have led to an absolute knowing that synchronicity is real, and a part of the mechanics of life – one way higher intelligence answers our needs. This incident triggered a personal insight into our role in belief.

March 2013, Salem: I am driving in town and thinking, as I often do in quiet moments, about coincidence. The familiar theme of the best ways to keep the "magic" going in particular. How can we live continuously in flow with its inherent synchronicities? A sign for the "Hollywood Station" post office seems to stand out. It feels somehow significant, but how?

I mull over the word "Hollywood," noting personal associations of pretense and make believe. That's what it means to me, I think, a place of movies, not truth. This bothers me. Are the coincidences we find meaningful simply products of our imaginations, instead of real messages from the Universe? No sooner do I have this doubting thought than the word "Hollywood," jumps out at me once again, this time from a sign naming a different place.

"Hollywood." I say the word aloud to myself. Suddenly I intuit that to experience the coincidental magic we must be willing to suspend our doubts. Be willing to believe what we see and hear. Get into the story. Just like we do at the movies.

Connection: From an initial idea that the world is connected, I've moved to an understanding. The Universe links things that need to be joined when and where they need it. Time and space are of no concern, as cosmic workings are unlimited; synchronicity included. People, words, and events will coincidentally come together as necessary.

This brings to mind how my friend Heather and her husband met. As a girl, she sometimes enjoyed watching the Rogue River flowing at the end of her street. Once she observed an interesting boy puttering around his yard on the other side.

Then, a decade later, she ran into him again, after coincidentally bumping his car. Now they've been together for many years. How fun that she could have a preview glimpse of her one and only, so long before he was. Then be at the right place much later to finally meet him!

Flow: From an initial inkling of the importance of flow, I've moved to a place of awe, Residing in this state is how our lives are supposed to be! I've discovered that following our intuition – our insights and coincidences – results in flow, the realm of happiness.

Whatever brings us joy, fulfillment and well-being is there. When we follow what feels right and most true in the moment we flow with the energy of life. And that connection with the force always feels good.

Becoming aware of synchronicity and benefiting from its guidance, changes each of us in different ways. Eric speaks of new realizations about his and the Universe's roles in obtaining wanted information or objects:

"Before the book research began, I was unaware of the essential role we play in coincidence. Then as Jenny started honing in on occurrences, I began to realize that I was personally causing stuff (synchronicities) to happen. For instance, my total focus over a stretch of time on a particular bike I could not afford, and then the money being there for it. Just one of many incidents that convinced me there was a connection.

"Now I am totally convinced that if we concentrate on something we can make it happen. But also things will sometimes align themselves even if we do not make a focused attempt. Sometimes just a casual desire for something will cause things to line up, when we're not paying attention, consciously anyway. Maybe the length of time we have held the desire has everything to do with it.

"And then there are the surprises – the incidents we realize we really wanted to happen if we look carefully at what we were doing before the coincidence, we can see our connection."

Deidre has also experienced changes after becoming aware of synchronicity, and its results. She writes me: "It's always a good idea to pay attention – and paying attention to life's coincidences had some interesting benefits. One observation I made was that coincidences occur really often.

"Coincidences enhance life by providing moments of humor, surprise, and wonderment. Life is quirky! Our ability to have fun and enjoy life's surprises helps us to be happy.

"On a much larger scale, paying attention to our choices helps us to make wise choices. Our move to New Mexico was a challenge – not everything went smoothly. However, the big decision to move was driven by an overpowering feeling of 'this is where we are supposed to be.' Events large and small kept popping up to confirm that our decision was the right one.

"My dear friend: my most recent quest for meaning began the day you approached me in the library and said we needed to be friends!" (We had met briefly before, then run into each other again. As we started getting reacquainted there was an immediate rapport between us, and surprise at mutual interests).

"Coincidentally," she continues, "I had checked out a yoga book for the first time with the intention of beginning a new health and fitness program. Little did I know that our friendship would grow and grow, and my exploration of yoga and Eastern philosophy would become the cornerstone of my inner life!

"Not a coincidence that you are the one person that is truly receptive to talking about this stuff! What a wonderful journey this is. I'm sure looking forward to many years on this meaningful less-traveled road."

20

Synchronicity – The Last Word

We've reached the end of this story, our tale of meaningful coincidence. We've strived to read its symbols – the words through which it's told. Though synchronicity speaks a language intended just for one, a perfectly personal, sometimes puzzling language. I began this quest with three important questions:

1) Do different types of personalities experience different types of coincidence?

2) Does one personality type experience mostly synchronicities involving written words; another type, spoken words? If so,

3) Will recognizing and understanding our special type of coincidence lead us to a happier and more meaningful life?

The bottom line is yes! The Universe speaks to us through coincidence, in uniquely private ways. We might think of its workings like this:

The WHAT: Our special synchronicities, sent through our favored sense-way of sight, sound, or occasionally action.

The WHEN: During our favorite or common activities.

The WHERE: Those places we do our favorite or regular things.

The HOW: Through written words if we prefer sight, through spoken words if we prefer sound, and through either type of words if we prefer action.

Of course, it's a given that these words will be unique words that are understandable and significant. Words that secretly convey shades of meaning original to us at the perfect moment and place. Words that answer our quest-ions – by coincidence.

And finally, there's the business of reason, the import-ant WHY of it all. Why does the Universe answer us through synchronicity? Though we will never know the answer to that for sure, we can certainly surmise, based on our own observations. Take a close look at the nature of this creative force that guides. When we do we will see the qualities of our benefactor reflected in every coincidence:

It's Real

Two days ago: I am working on this section in the last chapter of the book, thinking what's most important to include. For some reason or another, the words "golden threads" come to mind. I hesitate, consider my meaning of the term and jot that down. "Golden threads," I write, "threads of sparkly new ideas that lead to rich insights." OK. Now what? I'm not sure if this is even relevant here. But feel it *might* be. So simply save my notes.

Then I work on writing up stories for this part, on the reasons that syncs happen. Each reason has an accomp-anying story, but this one, "It's Real." After a while I decide to take a break and read awhile. I start a new book, *The*

Hand on the Mirror: A True Story of Life Beyond Death, by Janis Heaphy Durham.

A few chapters into the book, the author related an uncanny event that I've never heard of before. While relaxing in the tub, she saw actual golden threads floating in the air before her! It's a fascinating account and I'm most amazed to come across it right now. Then there's that little click of recognition as things suddenly make sense. *Here's* my example for the section I am writing (and you are reading), saying, *sure, you bet, it's real!*

It's Caring

May 2014, California: Deidre shares this thought-provoking incident of coincidental concern. "My sister Carol and her husband James had been best friends with Mary and Mike for nearly 50 years. The two couples even vacationed together, and thoroughly enjoyed each others' company. Although Mike had some serious health problems, the four of them planned to go on a New Zealand tour in the fall. A few months before the trip Mike died.

"Carol and James decided to go on the tour as planned, though somewhat sadly, without their good friends. They arrived in New Zealand, and found seats on the tour bus for the first leg of the trip. Then they heard a voice behind them that *sounded* so much like Mike!

"In the course of the tour, they got to know the man, who also *looked* a lot like Mike. They told him they had a close friend whom he reminded them of. Their new acquaintance said that, coincidentally, James reminded him of his best friend back home. Carol said that this guy's personality and sense of humor were so like Mike's that by the end of the trip they felt he had kind of gone with them."

It's Wise

June 2014, Corvallis OR: My sister Gayle tells of receiving some sound advice at a rough time. "My good friend Sue had died unexpectedly, and I was very sad. The two of us had been best friends for a long time, and become particularly close over the last few years.

"Even though we couldn't get together too often, we always had a ball when we did. Talking about anything and everything going on in our lives – listening and supporting each other. And just plain having fun with lots and lots of laughs.

"When I heard the sad news about her, I was completely devastated. I kept wondering if I could have done something to have prevented it from happening. But then everything was unexpected, so that was unlikely. I missed Sue so much – there just wasn't anyone else who could be as special of a friend.

"About that time, my grandson Jake and his girlfriend broke up. He was a teenager, and the two of us were very close. Jake was heartbroken, of course, and going through the misery of it all, and I really felt for him.

"Then he heard about Sue and called to cheer *me* up! When I asked how *he* was doing, he said, 'I'm okay now, Grandma. I decided to think about the good times my girlfriend and I had instead of being sad.'

"Wow! What wise words from someone so young! I recognized the message for myself too, and decided to do the same."

It's Generous

December 2012, Salem: Deidre shares this incident showing open-heartedness. "Adam and I were orchestrating our big move to New Mexico. Naturally many things, some simple and some complex, were involved. My mother had recently died, and an inheritance was coming as soon as the estate was settled.

"We had big plans for the money – to purchase our new home with it in New Mexico. And hoped the funds would arrive by a favorite time of ours, the winter solstice, which just happened to be the next day.

"In the morning I was excited to find that the first of two inheritance checks had arrived in the mail, along with, by chance, the first copy of a New Mexico travel magazine. We really felt encouraged with our moving plans, and the rightness of our decision to make them."

It's Fun

April 2015, Portland, OR: My son Jason, who works in property management, calls to tell me this fun coincidence. He explains, "We were replacing the outside tables and chairs from the decks at the hotel. The new sets had arrived a few days before, and I had been finding homes for the old ones. So far all but four of the original sets had been claimed by employees and their families.

"No one seemed to want the last few, so I called a couple guys who work as recyclers to pick them up in the morning. Then I locked them in the trash pick-up area. Here is where it gets strange. When I told my roommate Joe about them, he was excited, and wanted one of the tables to put where we barbecue. I hadn't thought of that. But it was really late – too late to call – and I had already set things up with the recyclers.

"In the morning I got to work early, hoping to call the guys before they came over. But it was too late and they had already come. Here's what is weird – for some reason or another they left *one* table behind. The other three tables were gone plus the chairs that went with them. But, by coincidence, a single table remained, just what we needed!"

It's Always There

January 2014, Salem: I'm heading to the local Goodwill for a little shopping. It's been a work day, and I'm looking forward to the break. As I drive I think about my morning's research on perimeters. More precisely, the question, are synchronicity's answers always available? I determine to be extra attentive, beginning right now, for a possible response. I don't have long to wait. At the store, the kitchenware aisle pulls, so I browse there first. A large display of mugs catches my attention and I stop to take a look. One in particular really seems to stand out. It's a big mug with a bold design and colorful lettering. I look closer and read its wording, so pertinent and meaningful. "Delivery," it promises, "24 Hours a Day, 7 Days a Week – Guaranteed!"

And there it is. Constant answers – always there.

My goals for this book were simple. To share my study of coincidence and its meaningful language of words. To serve as a possible catalyst for your own discoveries. I've relished the search, and been changed by what I've found. Maybe you have, too.

The final word of synchronicity? *Possibilities.* May we flow with our clear coincidences, may we explore the cryptic ones. For every synchronicity tells its own story through secret words or other clues, that when deciphered solve its mystery.

References

Chapter 1
Jung, C.G. *Synchronicity: An Acausal Connecting Principle.* (Princeton / Bollingen Paperback.). Princeton, New Jersey: Princeton University Press, 1973.

Chapter 2
Camp, Robert. *The Cards of Your DESTINY: Look Into Your Past, Present, and Future Using the Ancient and Original Science of Card Reading.* Tampa, Fl: Seven Thunders Publishing Company, 1992.

Richmond, Olney H. *The Mystic Test Book or the Magic of the Cards.* Chicago: (The Temple Publishing Company), 1893. Now in the public domain in the United States.

Chapter 3
May, Elaine, Screenwriter & Director, *A New Leaf.* Based on Jack Ritchie's Short Story "The Green Heart." Perfs. Walter Matthau, Elaine May. 1970. Videocassette. Paramount Pictures Corp., 1987.

Chapter 4
Jones, Jr., Henry Z. *Psychic Roots: Serendipity & Intuition in Genealogy.* Baltimore, MD: Genealogical Publishing Co., Inc., 1993.

Chapter 7

Morley, Christopher. *The Haunted Bookshop.* New York: Grosset & Dunlap, 1919. Now in the public domain in the United States.

MacLeod, Michael (1 December 2011). "Edinburgh book sculptures turn the page. The final chapter of a touching anonymous tribute to the power of words has just appeared." The Guardian.

Marsack, Robyn (31 July 2012). "Edinburgh's mysterious book sculptures go on tour." The Guardian.

Chapter 10

Farber, Monte, and Zerner, Amy. *The Zerner/Farber Tarot Deck.* NY: Zerner / Farber Editions, Ltd., 1997. www.TheEnchantedWorld.com.

Chapter 11

Moss, Robert. *The Three Only Things: Tapping the Power of Dreams, Coincidence, and Imagination.* Novato, California: New World Library, 2007. (From the book The Three Only Things. Copyright 2007, by Robert Moss. Reprinted with permission of New World Library, Novato, CA. www.newworldlibrary.com.).

Chapter 12

Shyamalan, M. Night, Screenwriter & Director, *Signs.* Perfs. Mel Gibson, Joaquin Phoenix. 2002. Television. November

2012.

Chambers, Ephraim. *Cyclopaedia, or, A Universal Dictionary of Arts and Sciences.* London, 1728. Now in the public domain of the United States.

Chapter 14

Thurston, Mark. *Synchronicity as Spiritual Guidance.* Virginia Beach, Virginia: A.R.E. Press, 1997.

Chopra, Doepak. *The Spontaneous Fulfillment of Desire: Harnessing the Infinite Power of Coincidence.* New York: Harmony Books, 2003.

Chopra, Doepak. *Daughters of Joy.* New York: G.P. Putnam's Sons, 2002.

Chapter 16

Ford, Jamie. *Hotel on the Corner of Bitter and Sweet: A Novel.* New York: Ballantine Books, 2009.

Moore, Thomas. *The Re-enchantment of Everyday Life.* New York: HarperCollins Publishers, 1996.

Chapter 20

Durham, Janis Heaphy. *The Hand on the Mirror: A True Story of Life Beyond Death.* New York, NY: Grand Central Publishing, 2015.

About the Author

Jenna Moore Fuller, a former vintage books dealer, has studied metaphysics for many years, with a special interest in synchronicity. She has written for websites and magazines, and kept longtime journals of her own meaningful coincidences along with those of family and friends.

After seeing the importance of words in coincidence, she focused on understanding its language. And discovered the different "styles" through which the Universe seems to speak to different people. *The Secret Language of Synchronicity* is an exploration of these types of guiding messages, along with the varying personal words that make them up.

Jenna currently is continuing her research into the phenomena (and collecting more stories!). She has learned that there's always more to learn about how the big U communicates with us through words we "happen" upon.

And one more thing from the author

When you turn the page after References, Kindle will provide an opportunity to rate this book and share your ideas on Facebook and Twitter. If you enjoyed it and want to share that, would you take a few minutes to let your friends know about it? They may be grateful and I know I will be! Also if you have found the book of value, a review on Amazon would be highly appreciated, too.

All the Best,
Jenna Moore Fuller

Made in the USA
San Bernardino, CA
11 May 2016